D1250675

50TH ANNIVERSARY

WOODSTOCK

BACK TO YASGUR'S FARM

MIKE GREENBLATT

FOREWORD BY COUNTRY JOE McDONALD

Fremont Public Library
1170 N. Midlothian Road
Mundelein, IL 60060

Copyright ©2019 F+W Media, Inc.

All rights reserved. No portion of this publication may be reproduced or transmitted in any form or by any means, electronic or mechanical, including photocopy, recording, or any information storage and retrieval system, without permission in writing from the publisher, except by a reviewer who may quote brief passages in a critical article or review to be printed in a magazine or newspaper, or electronically transmitted on radio, television, or the Internet.

Published by

Krause Publications, a division of F+W Media, Inc.
5225 Joerns Drive, Suite 2 • Stevens Point, WI 54481
715-445-2214 • 888-457-2873
www.krausebooks.com

To order books or other products call toll-free 1-855-864-2579
or visit us online at www.krausebooks.com

Grateful acknowledgment is made for permission to reprint the lyrics of:
"Bring Back the Sixties, Man," words and music by Joe McDonald, © 1978 Alkatraz Corner Music Co., BMI;
"Janis," words and music by Joe McDonald, © 1967 Joyful Wisdom Publishing, BMI;
"I-Feel-Like-I'm-Fixin'-To-Die Rag," words and music by Joe McDonald, © 1965 and renewed 1993 Alkatraz Corner Music Co., BMI.

ISBN-13: 978-1-4402-4890-0
ISBN-10: 1-4402-4890-7

Front cover (from left): Joe Cocker; Woodstock fans on VW Bus; and Joan Baez: AP photos

Designed by Dave Hauser
Edited by Paul Kennedy

Printed in China

10 9 8 7 6 5 4 3 2 1

contents

Image courtesy Bear Family Records

FOREWORD BY COUNTRY JOE McDONALD

A TIMELESS LOVEFEST

For three days in August of 1969 over one half million people attended an open-air concert held in a cow pasture on Max Yasgur's dairy farm in New York State. No one had ever seen such a thing before. The huge crowd was not expected by the promoters. They thought that maybe 50,000 people might come to their three-day event featuring over 30 pop/rock music acts that were popular with young people of the day. But over one half million young people converged on the tiny town of Bethel, New York. To the shock, dismay, joy and amazement of the town, the audience, and the world, an ocean of young people swarmed upon them. There were so many that collecting and selling tickets proved to be impossible turning it into a free festival. It was declared a disaster by the government but a lovefest by most all that attended.

Captured in Michael Wadleigh's Oscar-winning documentary Woodstock, Country Joe McDonald's impromptu solo performance became a generational moment.

The event was filmed by several film crews and recorded. And in spite of a torrential rain storm the film and recording survived. The music album sold millions and the film went on to achieve Academy Awards. Millions worldwide experienced both the film and recording, revealing a brand new culture that clashed with the dominant World War Two generation in ways that are still alive today.

Fifty years later it feels like déjà vu all over again. The status quo seems to desire an era that clashes with our dream of peace and love. Back then we struggled to change things so we could collectively live happy and healthy lives. Today we struggle for change not only for ourselves but also for our home, planet earth.

The problems we dealt with then still exist. And like back then, having hope for the future often seems impossible. But one thing has not changed. Music inspired us and soothed us and united us and gave us hope and today it can do the same.

As we pause to reflect upon the passage of fifty years since the Woodstock Music Festival, perhaps once again it can do for us what it did back then. Allow us all to have some fun as we work together toward our common goal, survival.

Happy Anniversary Woodstock!

Joe McDonald

COUNTRY JOE MCDONALD'S ROUSING SOLO ACOUSTIC VERSION OF "THE 'FISH' CHEER/I-FEEL-LIKE-I'M-FIXIN'-TO-DIE RAG" IS ONE OF THE MOST MEMORABLE PERFORMANCES AT WOODSTOCK. THE SONG, WITH ITS BITING SARCASM AND DARK HUMOR, BECAME A FAVORITE VIETNAM WAR PROTEST SONG.

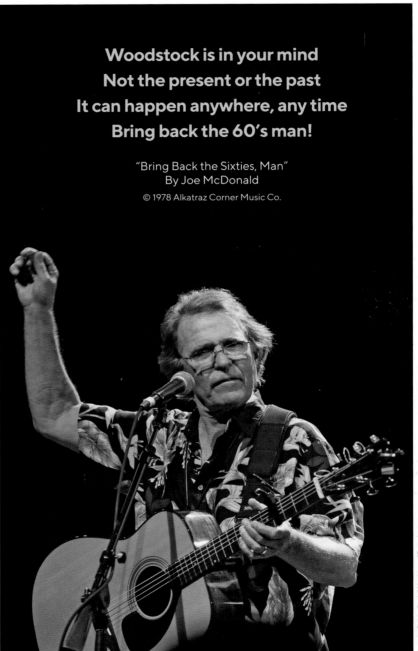

**Woodstock is in your mind
Not the present or the past
It can happen anywhere, any time
Bring back the 60's man!**

"Bring Back the Sixties, Man"
By Joe McDonald

© 1978 Alkatraz Corner Music Co.

Photo by Bobby Bank/WireImage/Getty Images

THE LINEUP

FRIDAY RICHIE HAVENS SWEETWATER BERT SOMMER TIM HARDIN RAVI SHANKAR MELANIE ARLO GUTHRIE JOAN BAEZ **SATURDAY** QUILL COUNTRY JOE McDONALD SANTANA JOHN SEBASTIAN KEEF HARTLEY BAND THE INCREDIBLE STRING BAND CANNED HEAT MOUNTAIN GRATEFUL DEAD CREEDENCE CLEARWATER REVIVAL JANIS JOPLIN SLY & THE FAMILY STONE THE WHO JEFFERSON AIRPLANE **SUNDAY** JOE COCKER & THE GREASE BAND COUNTRY JOE & THE FISH TEN YEARS AFTER THE BAND JOHNNY WINTER BLOOD, SWEAT & TEARS CROSBY, STILLS, NASH & YOUNG PAUL BUTTERFIELD BLUES BAND SHA NA NA JIMI HENDRIX

Photo by Daniel Wolf/The Boston Globe via Getty Images

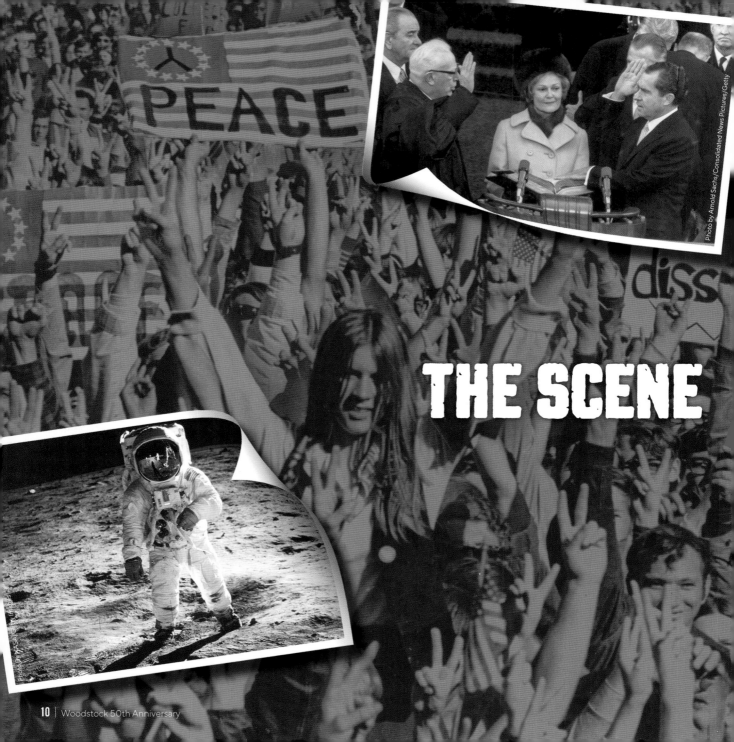

PEACE

THE SCENE

diss

Photo by Arnold Sachs/Consolidated News Pictures/Getty

On one long, mind-blowing late summer weekend in August of 1969 a three-day music festival was held on a farm in upstate New York. The concert starred some of the biggest names in rock history. Even so, the real show was the scene itself. By the end of the weekend, that beautiful, bizarre and implausible scene would define a generation.

Inspired by the artsy community of Woodstock, New York, a hub for artists of all stripes and where Bob Dylan had settled, The Woodstock Music & Art Fair – promising "3 Days of Peace & Music" – unfolded from August 15-17 in nearby Bethel. More than a music fest, it turned out to be a gathering of the tribes, a place to let it all hang out with no supervision whatsoever, to smoke pot, make love, go swimming and meet fellow antiwar hippies. Plus, the opportunity to enjoy one rock 'n' roll superstar after another under the sun and stars in a bucolic setting, on a farm with a lake, proved too much to pass up.

So they came...in numbers that were impossible to predict.

Michael Lang (a New York hippie entrepreneur who had staged the 1968 Miami Pop Festival) and his partner, music-biz executive Artie Kornfeld, with money from two independently wealthy venture capitalists (John Roberts and Joel Rosenman), set out to bring every great band in the world to one stage for one weekend. All four were young, in their twenties. And in for the ride of their lives.

Lang was smart enough to get some real professionals. Bill Hanley, known as "The Father Of Festival Sound," John Morris (who booked the bands) and the staff of the famed rock venue The Fillmore East, including NYU Professor Chris Langhart, effectuated Lang's vision. Fillmore East owner Bill Graham made phone calls vouching for Lang and one by one, starting with Creedence Clearwater Revival, the big time acts signed on.

Image courtesy Michael Stern

Welcome to Woodstock and the meeting of the tribes, called together to celebrate music and youth.

Image courtesy Heritage Auctions

America, in 1969, was torn apart by the war in Vietnam, Civil Rights and Women's Liberation. Nixon was in the White House, Armstrong was on the Moon and the seeds of revolution were in the air. Youth marched in the streets and on college campuses, openly rejecting the America of their parents' generation. They grew their hair long, smoked pot, listened to a different kind of music, and had a different set of heroes.

What Lang, Roberts, Rosenman, Morris, Hanley and Langhart couldn't possibly have envisioned was the influx of youth that streamed into the farm from all sides...and never stopped. They had no way of knowing that they'd set into motion a seismic, once-in-a-lifetime event that grew and grew with a life of its own as more and more kids flooded into the area.

They weren't prepared. But then again, how could they be?

When efforts to garner security with off-duty New York City cops fell through...when the gates were trampled over...when a whole city materialized in the 600-acre bowl in front of the stage, they knew they were in over their heads, declaring it a free concert. With not enough food, water, bathrooms, and minimal-to-no security, half a million people sat there peacefully in the rain Friday and Saturday in an idyllic setting on Max Yasgur's farm, awash in nudity, drugs and independence. Freedom! Free from the social constraints of existing laws, they made love, got high, grooved to the music and when the food ran out, and the site was declared a disaster area, the locals helped by showing up in flatbed trucks handing out bread, fruit, vegetables and peanut butter and jelly sandwiches.

The original Woodstock poster designed by David Byrd listed Wallkill, New York, as the concert site. That changed after residents freaked out over the idea of an army of hippies invading their town.

Then, on Sunday, a monsoon with almost tornado-like winds, whipped through the stoned masses. Almost four hours straight of nonstop rain fell violently from the heavens and stopped the concert dead in its tracks, soaking the kids to the bone. Then the temperatures plummeted. Yet these kids, despite the conditions, helped each other, fed each other, got each other high and kept each other warm, ultimately proving to the world that their "peace and love" mantra was real. Cops were confounded. They heard what was going on in their little town. Yet they left the kids alone. Despite New York Gov. Nelson Rockefeller wanting to send in National Guard troops to disperse the crowd, despite the rains eroding the soil atop underground electrical wiring, despite the daunting prospect of 500,000 cold, wet, hungry, thirsty kids jammed belly-to-butt in a solid downpour, there was not one isolated instance of reported violence. It is still, 50 years later, hard to believe.

It had never happened before.

It hasn't happened since.

The thrill of seeing Jimi Hendrix, Janis Joplin, Johnny Winter, Jefferson Airplane, Crosby, Stills, Nash & Young, Joan Baez and 26 other acts one after another was enough to mollify even the most disgruntled fan. The long delays in-between artists meant that the bigger acts didn't take the stage until ungodly hours of the morning. It didn't matter. Those who were there will remember it for the rest of the lives.

I know I will.

Kids flooded into Bethel, New York, as a seismic, once-in-a-lifetime event overwhelmed even the most ambitious imaginations.

Photo by Hulton Archive/Getty Images

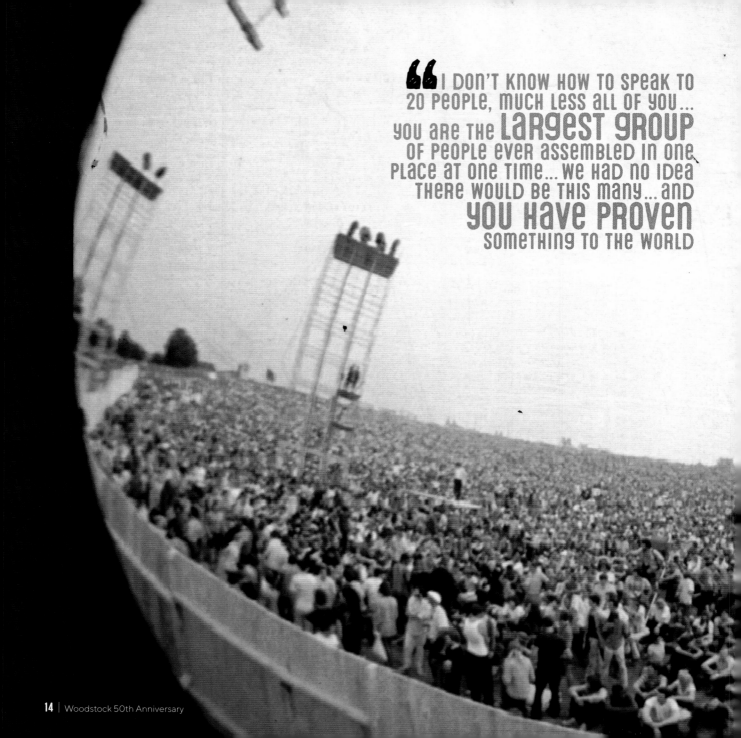

“ I DON'T KNOW HOW TO SPEAK TO 20 PEOPLE, MUCH LESS ALL OF YOU... YOU ARE THE **LARGEST GROUP** OF PEOPLE EVER ASSEMBLED IN ONE PLACE AT ONE TIME... WE HAD NO IDEA THERE WOULD BE THIS MANY... AND **YOU HAVE PROVEN** SOMETHING TO THE WORLD

...THAT HALF A MILLION KIDS CAN GET TOGETHER FOR FUN AND MUSIC AND HAVE NOTHING BUT FUN AND MUSIC. "

— Dairy farmer Max Yasgur, his voice breaking, addressing the massive Woodstock audience washing over the 600 acres of land he provided for the festival.

Photo by Ralph Ackerman/Getty Images

BROWN ACID BLUES

FIRST·AID

Photo by Bettmann/Getty Images

I'm sitting on the grass of a huge field of dreams. It's a beautifully sunny Sunday afternoon and we're excited to see Joe Cocker. My new friends—some 500,000 of them—are sitting with me. The drugs are starting to kick in, the pot and hashish I smoked, the warm red wine I drank, and, especially, the brown acid (LSD) I had just taken from a kindly elderly lady who also gave me bread. That's when the following announcement was made by the calm, reassuring voice of stage host Chip Monck.

The warning was blunt and dire. Don't take the brown acid. Did I hear right? I had just taken it! "You may take it with however many grains of salt that you wish," intoned Monck, "that the brown acid circulating around us isn't too good. It is suggested that you stay away. Of course, it's your own trip, so be my guest, but please be advised that there is a warning on that one, OK?"

Wet, hungry and tripping, Woodstock Nation turned to an overtaxed first aid station for reprieve. A Sunday afternoon storm temporarily dampened spirits and turned the festival into a mud bath.

Oh no! Would I survive the brown acid? Or would I be dragged kicking and screaming in a total psychotic state into the medical tent that was already overrun? Hell, I thought I was stronger than this. I had survived the draft by going to college and earning one of those treasured college deferments while my friends were getting sent against their will to fight an immoral and illegal war in Southeast Asia. Vietnam, Women's Liberation and Civil Rights were the pressing issues of the day. I had survived the 1967 Newark, New Jersey, race riots despite working in a little newsstand downtown on the corner of Broad and Market right where rioters threw rocks through store windows (one such looter went into his pocket for a quarter to buy the Newark Star-Ledger from me). That night, my mom and I stayed up late listening to the gunshots. Clinton Avenue was burning. I had also survived snorting some white powder in college called "doojie." It made me throw up. Little did I know it was heroin. I cleaned up the vomit and went back to doing my in-house radio show—which went as far as the Essex County College cafeteria—that I called "The Devil's Ass."

But this was different.

Joe Cocker's early Sunday afternoon set was a rousing time for a crowd soon to be soaked by a relentless storm.

Associated Press photo

Photo by Pictorial Parade/Hulton Archive/Getty Images

Inhibitions, as well as clothes, were cast aside throughout the weekend for many concertgoers awash in music and new-found freedom.

Photo by Silver Screen Collection/Getty Images

I was alone. Cocker's set was to be the opening salvo of rock 'n' roll under blue skies and warm vibes on the third and final day of the Woodstock Music and Arts Fair. My friend Neil had gone off in search of a phone booth to call our moms. The people around me quickly became my brothers and sisters against a cruel establishment who wouldn't let us 18-year olds vote but who had no compunction in sending us halfway around the world to die in some Vietnam rice paddy. The sense of brotherhood here was palpable. I felt safe, cocooned against the elements by the music and the feeling that we had been talking about all morning that the whole world was watching. We knew this. We were, indeed, changing the world, proving our point. We had verbalized throughout the night how the sixties were the cut-off point of everything that had gone on before. Make Love Not War. If it feels good do it. Reality is a crutch. We even used to wear buttons saying such hippie bromides and we believed them.

But where the hell was Neil?

I was starting to feel a little paranoid. Cocker's exciting set came and went but when it got dark in the middle of Sunday afternoon and my friend still wasn't there, the brown acid started to really kick my ass, and the people all around me seemed to be not that friendly anymore. Some of their faces seemed to be melting. And a whole new set of people seemed to be crowding in on me from all sides. How could they all be so well dressed? Did they just get here? I felt like they were looking down on me in my dirty T-shirt and shorts that I wore for days.

> *How could it get so dark in the middle of the afternoon? The wind started whipping around like crazy hoisting garbage up, up and away. The people around me were stony silent. The good vibes seemed like yesterday. Nobody was sharing water, food and pot anymore.* **C'mon man!**

How could it get so dark in the middle of the afternoon? The wind started whipping around like crazy hoisting garbage up, up and away. The people around me were stony silent. The good vibes seemed like yesterday. Nobody was sharing water, food and pot anymore. C'mon man! This was the same spot I'd been in since arriving early on Thursday! Could the cast of characters have changed so profoundly? Who were these new people?

My need for water and food (and toothpaste) was making me nervous. I cringed away from my new neighbors toward this big bear of a man wearing a holster for his long knife, his hair braided, his tattoos totally pornographic and his hairy belly protruding out from his dirty jeans inches more than what would be usually be deemed morbidly obese. Back in Newark, I'd be scared to hell of this guy. But here? I felt a kinship. He was laughing, not judging me, and he was generous and he was tending a warm fire and giving out joints and tootsie rolls. He told me Dylan was still going to show up and got me all excited. Everywhere you went, people were saying how Dylan was going to show up. At the moment I would've been satisfied just having Neil show up.

The brown acid now totally took over. Perhaps if the music had continued after Joe Cocker, and the weather would've been nice, with the continuing largesse of our neighbors, and my friend Neil at my side, I could've would've should've dug the scene. We still had the blanket left for us by a pair of sisters from Delaware who kept telling us that they were witches and students of the dark arts. When they left, sometime Saturday night, their blanket stayed

As Sunday morning broke, concertgoers embraced a new day and a new reality.

Associated Press photo

Photo courtesy Michael S

With 500,000 tightly-packed neighbors, the festival proved to be the ultimate shared experience.

behind. Now they were gone, Neil was gone, I was tired after not having slept for three of those four days, and I was thirsty, wet, hungry, cold and had to go to the bathroom.

The only thing emanating from the stage was silence. More and more people around me got naked (they were smart and were storing their clothing under tarps). The rain was pissing down on us heavy. Our great spot right in front

of the stage had turned into a cold brown lake. It was time to move but how would Neil ever find me if I did? I noticed some Hells Angels types building fires for warmth and sharing an industrial-sized can of cold Raviolios, which they were doling out from one huge wooden spoon to starving hippies like myself. I got in line and damn if those cold Raviolios weren't the greatest thing I ever tasted. I made my way back to the end of the line for another hit.

Settling against a tree, which provided some small semblance of dryness, I watched a couple make love in the mud. Or was it real? I was tripping my brains out and realized then that they weren't making love; they were doing some kind of weird yoga in different positions and singing in a foreign language. Rumors of locals pulling up in flatbed trucks with food started circulating but I was still trapped in a sea of humanity close to the stage and didn't want to go too far from our spot because I knew Neil was trying to find his way back to me.

"I was sitting against a tree meditating," Neil told me 48 years later.

Fans soon discovered that if they listened to the music all would be revealed.

Photo by Archive Photos/Getty Images

The silence from the stage was deafening. If only the music would start. Then everything would be alright. The concept of music-as-salvation started for me at Woodstock. As long as the music was playing, we were good. The music was everything. That mindset has permeated my entire concert-going life. And it all stems from Woodstock. It matters not at concerts today what is going on around me as long as the music is playing, I can reach a musical state of Zen. Because of Woodstock, I have learned the important life-lesson to just listen to the music...and all will be revealed. Nowadays, the reality is, of course, that the person sitting next to you is not your brother. At Woodstock, though, he or she was. And sometimes they even took their top off.

Neil still wasn't back. Was I even in the same spot? The close relationship to the stage had always been our divining rod and when people started planting flags close to us, we used those visuals to find our way back. Hell, I had even gone skinny-dipping yesterday, throwing my T-shirt, shorts, underpants and sneakers on the ground. Should they be stolen, I'd have to find the car...wherever the hell it was. I was glad my clothing was still there after my close encounter with an angel in the lake. She had a lovely smile. I think she liked that I was openly staring at her. I think we kissed but I'm not sure. I'll never forget her. I never even got her name.

But now the rain wouldn't stop. There still was no music and no Neil. And I seemed to be tripping even harder than I was a few hours ago. It was official survival mode. This was not fun anymore.

Damn the brown acid. Damn the rain. And damn Neil. It was never supposed to be like this...

CHAPTER ONE

AND OFF
WE WENT

e weren't going to go. Led Zeppelin was playing down the shore in Asbury Park, New Jersey, but the Woodstock Music & Arts Fair in Bethel, New York, Sullivan County, Catskill Mountains, kept calling to my good friend Neil Yeager and myself via radio commercials. The FCC, in 1966, had mandated different programming for AM and FM radio. Prior to '66, you heard the same thing on both frequencies. Now, legally bound to offer new sound, FM radio became a harbinger for hearing new music, underground music, music of the burgeoning counterculture. Thus, WOR-FM and WNEW-FM became almost religious to us pot-smoking hippies. The ads insisted we be there. How could we not? So it was bye-bye Zep when I walked into The Last Straw in Bloomfield, New Jersey, to plunk down $17.50 for my three-day pass to the fest.

And off we went.

Author Mike Greenblatt.

Jefferson Airplane, at the time of our Thursday, August 14, 1969 departure, were sequestered in a Holiday Inn close to the site, having come in Wednesday from a Pennsylvania show. "We had been watching news reports on television all the while getting updates from various folks," remembers bassist Jack Casady. "We knew we were up against it. Luckily, everybody else—all the artists—were also staying at that hotel. The stage was still being built a day before the festival on Thursday. It was all so new. And big. The amount of people who just flooded into the area in droves totally took us by surprise. They were out there in all directions. The news considered it a total phenomenon what with the presence of all the alternative people. All these building materials had to be brought in and a phalanx of sound guys, lighting

Image courtesy Heritage Auctions

Woodstock Music and Art Fair | Woodstock Music and Art Fair | Woodstock Music and Art Fair

| THREE DAY TICKET |

FRIDAY
August 15, 1969
10 A. M.
$6.00
Good For One Admission Only
79909 NO REFUNDS

SATURDAY
August 16, 1969
10 A. M.
$6.00
Good For One Admission Only
79909 NO REFUNDS

SUNDAY
August 17, 1969
10 A. M.
$6.00
Good For One Admission Only
79909 NO REFUNDS

THREE DAY TICKET
Aug. 15, 16, 17 1969
$18.00
79909

An unused three-day ticket to the greatest concert in history.

Kids wore their heart on their sleeves – and on their cars – as they headed off to Woodstock.

guys, construction workers, musicians, crews, hangers-on, managers and more made us go in Friday when we weren't even supposed to play until Saturday."

Bill Hanley, known as "The Father of Festival Sound," was already hard at work, living in a trailer behind the stage, nestled within the 600 acres of Max Yasgur's dairy farm. Hanley had mixed sound at the Newport Jazz Festivals for promoter George Wein since 1957. He worked the soundboards at the two Miami Pop festivals in 1968, as well as the Atlantic City Pop Festival just two weeks prior to Woodstock. The festival was the brainchild of Florida head-shop entrepreneur Michael Lang who had co-produced the Miami Pop Festival in May of 1968. "I knew Michael wanted good audio," remembers Hanley, "and I wanted the artists to be happy with their sound. I had a pretty good idea of what had to be done but knew it wouldn't be easy. Little did I know just how hard it would be. Still, I knew I could do it." Hanley would go on to design and lay out the sound system and the stage area, and is credited with making sure the people at the top of the hill heard every note while not blasting out those in front. And he did it beautifully.

"Originally," he says, "Michael called just to ask me how to do it all. I wouldn't tell him so he had to hire me. We became best of friends after that. He tried to beat me down price-wise, and he did, because I really wanted to do it." He did it so well that Richie Havens told reporters it was the best outdoor sound he had ever encountered.

Blissfully unaware of what Neil and I were heading toward, the Thursday ride up north from New Jersey was filled with good vibes. We kept shouting out the names of the acts we wanted to see. Jimi Hendrix! Johnny Winter! Sly & The Family Stone! The Band! Mountain! Canned Heat! We had just seen Santana at the site of the 1964 World's Fair in Flushing, Queens, New York, at a venue called The Singer Bowl, opening for Buddy Miles and a band called Pacific Gas & Electric. Santana blew my mind that night and I couldn't wait to see them again. We also had just seen Sly at a small Greenwich Village dungeon of a club in a basement called The Cafe Wha? and was totally thrilled when Jimi Hendrix jumped onstage to jam out with Sly on "I Want To Take You Higher." We had been waiting to get in when we saw Jimi stroll right past us with a gorgeous blonde on his

arm who looked like a Swedish super-model.

We also talked politics. A lot of politics. The '60s were a time where if you saw another longhair on the street, that longhair was your brother, and you could safely assume he was against the war in Vietnam.

photo by Three Lions/Getty Images

Image courtesy Heritage Auctions

Designer Arnold Skolnik's Woodstock poster.

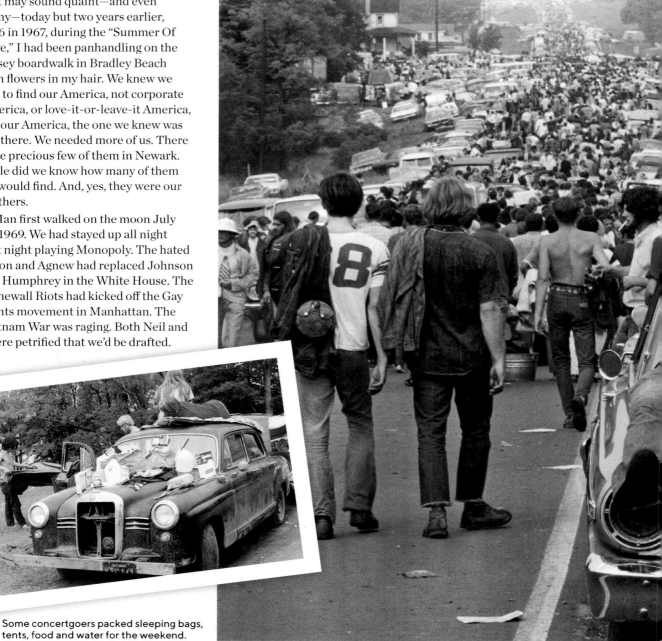

It may sound quaint—and even corny—today but two years earlier, at 16 in 1967, during the "Summer Of Love," I had been panhandling on the Jersey boardwalk in Bradley Beach with flowers in my hair. We knew we had to find our America, not corporate America, or love-it-or-leave-it America, but our America, the one we knew was out there. We needed more of us. There were precious few of them in Newark. Little did we know how many of them we would find. And, yes, they were our brothers.

Man first walked on the moon July 20, 1969. We had stayed up all night that night playing Monopoly. The hated Nixon and Agnew had replaced Johnson and Humphrey in the White House. The Stonewall Riots had kicked off the Gay Rights movement in Manhattan. The Vietnam War was raging. Both Neil and I were petrified that we'd be drafted.

Some concertgoers packed sleeping bags, tents, food and water for the weekend.

Photo courtesy Michael Stern

On foot, in cars, atop cars, people found their way to Woodstock. Some even managed to find sleep over the weekend.

Bettmann/Getty Images

Should we go to Canada? What if they abolish the college deferment? The murderous Manson Family just made headlines and the newspapers were quick to try and kill the hippie dream. We knew the hippie dream was alive and well, that we could—and would—change the world, and that our generation was the cut-off point from all previous generations. We were self-styled revolutionaries. We waved our freak flag high. We just needed to find the rest of us.

The truth was that we were suburban kids playing at revolution because it was trendy. We were weekend-hippies who would gobble blotter acid and drive into the city to see shows at the Fillmore East. Little did we know that it would be that same Fillmore East sound and lighting crew that would make Woodstock possible.

One of those Fillmore East sound guys was Chris Langhart, Woodstock's Technical Director/Designer. He had arrived on the scene with most of the crew, which had formed with John Morris at The Anderson Theater by Bill Graham. You can call him the MVP of Woodstock. He was responsible for the backstage area, the medical tent, the free kitchen and the VIP area. He even built the bridge that the artists walked on so they wouldn't have to walk through thousands of concertgoers since backstage was, in actuality, across the road behind the massive stage. Langhart had met Lang at the Fillmore East when Woodstock was just a twinkle in the curly-headed young man's eye. Woodstock was his vision. His baby. Being the Fillmore East's main tech guy and also an NYU college professor, Hanley knew he wanted him to realize his sound vision. After traveling down to Florida to see what Hanley did in Miami the

year before, he made some designs for the original Wallkill site, which Lang rejected. ("I don't think they were rustic enough for his tastes," says Langhart, "I was more into modern design.") That Wallkill, New York, stage was never built anyway. The locals there wanted nothing to do with a hippie festival and soon dairy farmer Max Yasgur entered the scene and offered his land in nearby Bethel.

The sleepy little hamlet of Bethel could only be entered by a one-lane highway, Route 17B. Neil and I were on the road! And we were thrilled! The back of the car was filled with two sleeping bags, a tent, sandwiches from my mom, two filled canteens, clothing, toothbrush, toothpaste, a transistor radio, Monopoly and books by Roth, Mailer, Miller, Vonnegut and Hesse. Did we really think we'd get any reading done?

Then the ride stopped. Dead. In the middle of nowhere. We turned off the car and waited – for hours. We even set up the Monopoly game on the roof of the car and started playing under the hot sun. Eventually, the cars started moving, and, after what seemed like a whole day, with the help of signs, we found the site, and were directed to a parking area, which seemed to be the highest point on a fairly large hill. I rolled a joint and we discussed the idea of walking all the way to the stage area with our tent, sleeping bags, canteens, extra clothing and a few books. Ultimately, it seemed easier to scope out the place first so we set off with nothing but the clothes on our back and the one joint. We figured we'd come back for our stuff.

That never happened.

We soon chanced upon a Volkswagen Beetle with a bunch of hippies inside, stuffed like too many clowns in a circus car. We were standing on the side of the one road down the mountain with our thumbs out and they stopped, laughing like crazy, telling us to stand on the running sideboards with our hands inside the windows so we wouldn't fall off. With slight hesitation, we did just that and the VW took off like a bat out of hell with Neil and I screaming for our lives until the car got to the bottom of the hill and zoomed to a stop. That's when we fell. Getting up, dusting ourselves off, we thanked our hosts and walked off to look for America.

The stage was still beset with scurrying workmen. It was Woodstock Eve. Chris Langhart was dealing with a myriad of problems and still waiting for the 100 phone booths that had to be shipped in. "As the site person," he remembers, "I had to see how the whole thing was ultimately organized. One of the things we needed was a way for

Peace out, man, proved a good philosophy while managing traffic into Bethel.

Photo by Ralph Ackerman/Getty Images

Unimagined crowds challenged expectations and overflowed garbage cans.

Photo by Daniel Wolf/The Boston Globe via Getty Images

everybody to call home so we needed pay phones. But we were in the middle of a farm field so it was necessary to call vendors and operate like a civilized purchasing operation. Thirty phones were brought in for the backstage area. We petitioned Ma Bell, made offers to pay, but nothing happened. My friend Tom Grimm was an employee of the phone company so I called him and he told me, 'if you pay, they have to serve you.' He called his superiors, I assume, and all of a sudden, seven trucks came down from Canada to lay seven miles of cable within a week, and we had backstage phones, pay phones and phone service. That enabled what—in essence—was the second largest city in the state of New York not to be the disaster that Life magazine would've portrayed, had not everybody called home to say what a great time they were having.

Neil and I had tickets in hand but there was no one to give them to so we threw them away and I lit the joint. Neil was in a straight phase and stayed sober for the next four days. I wanted to get high but still thought I had to hide the fact that I was smoking a joint in public so I went behind a tree to toke up. Eventually, we found the stage. It was massive. So exciting! We slapped each other five and joined a few like-minded souls on the grass so close to the stage that we could see the facial expressions of the workers still setting up for tomorrow morning's first note.

As the darkness enveloped us, I got stoned on OPD (other people's dope) and as more and more people crowded in on us, we learned for the first time how to take up as much space as possible. We certainly didn't want to upset

Bettmann/Getty Images

Arlo Guthrie declared "The New York State Thruway's closed, man!" He wasn't far off as traffic into town ground to a halt.

the friendly folks who were constantly sharing their water, wine, food, pot and hashish.

When Neil reminded me that it might be a good idea to make the trek back to the car and get our supplies for the weekend. In truth, we both knew that we'd never make it back to the car to get our stuff. Hell, we didn't even know where the car was. We'd have to survive on the largesse of our neighbors, that, and the few hot dog stands still being erected. Then someone pulled out a Monopoly board! We wound up playing Monopoly by flashlight for the rest of the night, finally conking out on the grass as the sun rose.

Meanwhile, Langhart had another problem on his hands: water. "Max [Yasgur] and I got on famously since I understood his milking and refrigeration systems as I lived next to a farm. I also renovated the air conditioning system at the Fillmore East. For the water system we bought trailer loads of PVC pipe and started trenching, though much piping ran on the surface. We installed seven wells pumping water into four 10,000-gallon holding tanks. Then came the problem of making the water pure because the state health department was insisting on this. They proposed a gas chlorinator, which I would not allow on the site for safety reasons. We opted instead to use thiazine pellets distributed in the piping as part of the purification system but they were bitter and unfortunately made the water taste like chlorine. Eventually, though, it all diluted and with the water filtered from the lake, we had enough. We had crews of diggers, drillers, and with [Production

Coordinator/Booker/Co-Host] John Morris's wife Ann keeping a tally of payroll so everyone got paid, at least 125 site crew people worked for days in my section alone. New York State kindly lent us several flatbed trucks of emergency water system parts that arrived incomplete. The piping was fairly obvious but the pumping part wasn't there. They provided thick instruction books that would've taken too long to figure out. In the end, we told the trucks to go back to wherever they came from."

Bill Hanley was otherwise occupied as well. "I had all I could do just to keep it all up and running. My main concern was that something would blow up. I had built a new console, found out it didn't work so I had to, essentially, punt." Hanley wound up overseeing the master recordings with a staff of ten, one of which, the late Lee Osborne, won an award for his sound work on the 1970 Woodstock movie. "We were working on a very low budget. I wish I had tape-delay but that cost too much and there was nowhere to rent one. There's also special stuff for permanent installation when you put a string of speakers down from the stage area every hundred feet or so all the way to the end of the audience. I would normally place speakers like spokes in a bicycle, with the spokes going out according to the lay of the land."

But he couldn't do that at Woodstock.

As more and more people showed up from all directions, our little area in front of the stage started getting crowded but we, unlike Langhart, didn't mind. Langhart soon realized this was going to be more, much more, than he

All the bands were very gracious. I remember Janis Joplin as being so sweet, so nice. In fact, I was supposed to go out on the road with her doing her sound before she accidently overdosed on heroin.
— BILL HANLEY

signed up for. "Well before the concert, people showed up offering to work. We picked workers by the look on their faces and few questions," he says now with a laugh. "Whoever looked the most sensible, we gave them chores like laying plywood floors for the medical tent. The next day some of those chosen became crew heads and more were added. We chose a local electrician whose son helped us hire non-union electrical workers and that was key to keeping expenses down, especially when utility transformers had to be installed at several places on the site. We did have some electrical ground leakage and a few people on stage got mildly electrocuted one afternoon during the rain, but it really wasn't so bad, no serious danger, just a slight tingle. I mean, you don't want to stand on a wet stage in your stocking feet and hold on to a microphone stand that is grounded somewhere else. There was never any high-voltage that got out of hand.

"We ran the second largest air force in the state with regard to the twenty-plus helicopters we used to get the artists in and out. At night, though, the pilots couldn't see where to land on the site. So we put Christmas tree lights around the fencing of the helipad area. It turned out to be one of the most egregious mistakes I ever made, because it was way too close to the performer pavilion. All the potential interviews that could've taken place with the performers and the press got obliterated by the sound of the copters! Once we were aware of it, there were so many people settled in all over the place, there was no way to relocate the landing area."

"All the bands were very gracious," adds Hanley. "I remember Janis Joplin as being so sweet, so nice. In fact, I was supposed to go out on the road with her doing her sound before she accidently overdosed on heroin. I had done sound at the Fillmore East so I knew a lot of the acts from there. As a matter of fact, light man Chip Monck, John Morris and I were the ones who convinced Bill Graham to open the Fillmore East. I had to keep seeing if the sound was loud enough to get all the way up the hill. We couldn't do a delay unit so I had to build special speakers. I would've paid out of my own pocket for the proper accouterments but then I'd be totally broke."

A view from the back of the Woodstock stage with the crowd filling the grounds while crew members hang lights and ready the Joshua Light Show backdrop.

Photo courtesy Amalie R. Rothschild

Morris ran the Fillmore East for Bill Graham. Always "the adult in the room," according to Josh White of the Joshua Light Show, Morris proved indispensable to Woodstock after Graham gave the festival his staff. He booked the bands, co-hosted the show from the stage and constantly put out fires. One such fire was Friday when he had to spend much of the first day of the festival on the phone with the Governor of New York Nelson Rockefeller's Chief of Staff who was talking about sending the troops in to clear the area.

"I remember arguing very forcefully that we knew what we were doing," says Morris. "We would control it. We'd be okay, and I got the guy to agree so they left us alone. They didn't send in the troops. They did later send some National Guard medical units, which were really helpful, and there was a moment, I think, on Sunday, when National Guard helicopters flew in over the crowd and you could hear their dramatic noise and I thought, 'uh-oh, we gotta be careful about this.' I knew they were Medevac Units so I said, 'ladies and gentlemen, the United States Army Medical Corps is here to help us,' and there was a gigantic BOO loud enough to almost knock the copters out of the air. So it was just a matter of attempting to turn everything into the area of communal cooperation of everyone working together."

Less than a year after Woodstock, President Nixon would send in the National Guard to quell a peaceful Kent

Only days before the concert was to start, workers scrambled to finish construction of the stage.

Photo courtesy Michael Stern

State antiwar protest. It would prove to be a fatal error. The American National Guardsmen shot four American students dead. Then, less than a year after that, Rockefeller sent in troops to quell a riot at Attica Prison with the disastrous result of thirty-three dead prisoners and ten dead correctional officers. Could you imagine what might have happened had not John Morris convinced the Governor's office not to send in the troops to disperse the crowd at Woodstock?

"Attica and Kent State were ridiculous decisions," says Morris. "Those of us who felt we were professional enough to deal with what we were dealing with, understanding the situation better than they did, felt that was the way to go. No troops. So that's what I tried to portray. I'm no hero. I'm just a guy who deals with logistics."

The only difference between this city and every other city in the country was that this city had no police force. A deal for off-duty New York cops to act as security fell through. The 500,000-plus all pitched in and helped each other, fed each other, and administered to each other's medical needs, at least by showing them the way to the med tent. There was no violence, no murder, no rape, not even a reported fight, which is absolutely amazing when you consider the elements and the lack of food, water and bathrooms.

It could never happen again.

Wade Lawrence, director and curator of The Museum of Bethel Woods, which now proudly stands on the exact spot that the festival took place, says, "I would love to believe it could happen again but the evidence suggests otherwise. The Museum has law enforcement documents—official records from police and health inspectors—about sunburn, sun stroke, cut feet and so on.

It runs some twenty pages and is summed up at the end in the final analysis with no reported instances of human-on-human violence. Woodstock represented young people coming together recognizing their oneness with one another, realizing that they could create a society—at least ideally—that wasn't their parents or mainstream society, that was peaceful and for a good purpose. I think the fact that the people created the festival with all the hardships be it rain, traffic, sanitation issues and everything and still rose above that without any real outside leadership or enforcement, spontaneously deciding to make it work, that right there epitomizes the '60s: the power of the people. The power of young people, people with conscience who could effect change without some government or military telling them to. This is why fifty years later Woodstock still resonates as that symbol of change.

"Look at American societal problems back then. Vietnam, Civil Rights, Women's Liberation, Gay Rights. They were all outside of the white Anglo-Saxon Protestant male top-of-the-pyramid ideal. The '60s changed all that. It was the first time we realized that there was a whole rainbow of people with validity who could contribute. It may have been but an ideal back then but it's come to fruition. It's law now. True, some of the political issues are very much still alive but the Baby Boomer Generation who are in their 60s today can look back at the 1960s and know a lot of what we argued for was true. We've been vindicated. Still, young people today may see that as ancient history. But they're still dealing with the same damn issues! To their credit, a lot of young people today are picking up the banner. Look at the 'Me Too'

movement. Look at the Women's March. Look at 'Black Lives Matter.' The intent of standing up for your rights, for equality, shows you cannot trust your political leaders. The people have to make their voices heard. And that, right there, was what the '60s were all about."

Jacob Cohen is a Chinese-Greek-Jew from Newark, one of my running buddies from the old neighborhood. His sister Luna was my first love. His father Joseph was a soldier in the Greek Army, a tailor,

Jacob Cohen

a shoemaker who left his family in 1938 Greece with his brother to escape the Nazis. Ending up in China, he met and married a beautiful young girl in Shanghai, had three children, got divorced, and brought his children to America where he had no visible means of supporting them so they ended up in foster homes. Joseph then rounded them up and moved with them directly upstairs from me, my mom and my grandparents in a small apartment house in Newark, where his brother Maurice would practice his electric bass guitar at all hours of the night and my grandfather would bang on the roof with a broom.

"The buildup to Woodstock was out-of-this-world," Jacob Cohen says. "There was never anything like it. Like frogs being boiled, we were in it, but we didn't know what was going on. During the race riots we saw the tanks coming through Weequahic Park. The riots prevented me from seeing Jimi Hendrix in '67 even though I had tickets. No

Michael Lang, the co-creator of Woodstock, rides his motorcycle through the camping area as people set up tents and lie on the grass prior to the festival opening.

Photo by Ralph Ackerman/Getty Images

Photo courtesy Amalie R. Rothschild

Technical director/designer Chris Langhart.

everything had to be done in a hurry. I had frequent contact with the partners: [Financier] Joel Rosenman would zoom up in his green Porsche and I would say, 'Go negotiate with the lady in that house because we are about to put up a water station or utility pole in her front yard.' Later he would return and say, 'that was bad...I could have bought the place for $5,000 and now I have to pay more than that just to put a pole in the yard.' There was no centralized management at the top, because we were all about the same age and there was a certain 'get it done' attitude and trust prevailing so when I said, 'there is only one person I know who can connect the tanks to the rest of the pipe system without instruction,' they said, 'why isn't he here?' to which I replied, 'because he's in California and so they flew him in straight away, no questions.

"In the audience area there was a small trailer with a 4- or 8-track recording system," Langhart says. "After his performance, Ravi Shankar's manager came into the recording trailer and decided he deserved to take the original tape reels away and somehow he did so. That's why there's a separate Ravi Shankar soundtrack rather than Shankar being part of the Woodstock soundtracks. There was no tape! Possession being nine-tenths of the law, we couldn't do anything about it.

"Backstage, I designed a tent for the performers and the construction was headed up by Richard Hartman. The live sound mixing was done out in the audience but one had to climb onto the stage to see which microphones were working. We had no quick access to the stage for sound persons, so invariably, the wrong microphone was plugged in every once in a while, but not often."

"Michael Lang felt secure with me," sound man Hanley says. "He knew I was totally prepared. I built special speakers. I had those towers built. As far as the elements were concerned, when the rains came, we threw out the polyethylene, iced things down when they invariably heated up and waited it out. We had to get through to the end of the show without any major disas-

way was I going to go downtown to see Jimi. Then Martin Luther King and Robert Kennedy were killed in '68. So Woodstock in '69 represented a beacon of hope. Peace and love, man. Plus sex and drugs. Growing up in such an era of turmoil proved ultimately to be a really magical time. Hearing about Woodstock over and over again on the radio was a calling so I knew I had to go.

"My friend Saul Mandel and I left Friday night. Got there real late. Joan Baez had already finished. We took his brother Paul's two-door 1965 Chevy Impala. There was heavy traffic. We found the first parking we could and immediately went to sleep in the car."

"There were plenty of planning errors, of course," admits Chris Langhart, "since we were pressed for time and ters. There wasn't much I could do after realizing my estimate of 100,000 [people] would only be 20% of the crowd. I only had 30 days to build those speakers and knew that the people all the way in the back could hear, if not see. It was an uphill battle all the way, but I had been battling with people all over the country to spend more money on audio. It was only when rock 'n' roll first started being taken seriously, and the musicians themselves asserted more control, did the demand go up for high quality sound. I was out there promoting high quality sound right from the beginning. Only difference was, now I was being listened to."

Hanley had a hand in picking the site based on the terrain. He designed the fencing and got along great with Lang, who, he says, "had good vibes about him. He was trying to make it right for all the right reasons. My mission was to make it happen and keep it going. My brother was doing sound for Cream right around the same time. I'll never forget how well behaved the kids were at Woodstock. That is the one thing that stands out in my mind. I mean, man, it could have been a total disaster."

> I'll never forget how well behaved the kids were at Woodstock. That is the one thing that stands out in my mind. I mean, **man, it could have been a total disaster.**
> — BILL HANLEY

The stage at bottom right is dwarfed by the massive crowd that spreads out across Max Yasgur's fields like so much wheat.

AP Photo/Marty Lederhandler

CHAPTER TWO

BEFORE THE FIRST ACT

ime can distort as easily as funhouse mirrors. The passage of decades tends to stretch and reshape events, sometimes beyond recognition. That's why historian Wade Lawrence wants to be clear about something.

"No one went to Woodstock to protest war," says Lawrence, of the Museum at Bethel Woods. "They came to have a good time and party to some great music in a rural setting with like-minded people. I think what happened during those four days was that a spotlight was shone on those ideals that were on the minds of young people. Those ideals had legs. There was something intrinsically right and good about treating your fellow man as your brother.

"You could make a statement while still getting stoned out of your mind and getting down to the music simultaneously. The fact that so many people got together as one and were peaceful is one very powerful political statement."

Legendary rock concert promoter Bill Graham [1931-1991] summed up the 1960s in his *Bill Graham Presents: My Life Inside Rock and Out* autobiography with Robert Greenfield. "Before this time," he writes, "there always were pockets of people in our society seeking alternative lifestyles. In the '60s, the funnel opened wide. For the first time in modern history, there was social upheaval among the young. The children. The world of people between 14 and 25. That didn't happen in the '30s. That was an economic upheaval. People may have rejected the existing order before but the difference this time was in the sheer strength of numbers. The vehicle was music. And millions of young people got on the bandwagon."

Graham died in a helicopter crash while coming home from a mission of mercy. He was 60, trying to get Huey Lewis to agree to perform a benefit for the victims of the 1991 Oakland Hills firestorm. His book came out posthumously in 1992. No other single person affected the course of live music in America as much as Graham. And he had a lot to do with the success of Woodstock in an unofficial capacity, not only coming up with the San Francisco bands who played, but with the architects of the festival itself who all worked for him at the Fillmore East. Including Chip Monck.

STAN HONDA/AFP/Getty Images

Wade Lawrence, the museum director and senior curator at The Museum at Bethel Woods.

Stage Lighting and Technical Designer Chip Monck was busy at Woodstock with the only things that were of interest to him: the stage, the audio support scaffolding and four follow-spot light towers in the audience area. All went up as the first order of business. Monck paid little attention to anything but his work.

"I didn't have to face the audience until Michael Lang announced backstage in no uncertain terms, 'we forgot to get an emcee!' It was 7 o'clock Friday morning so as the roof of the stage was being built, I was duly informed that the audience was my responsibility as well as the lighting," Monck recalls. "That's when I noticed the enormity of that audience. There were, uh, a few more than I expected."

Then Lang told Monck that the largest throng of kids he had ever seen assembled in one place needed to move back from the stage another 20 feet or so for safety reasons. So, mildly terrified, Monck began to talk to the audience for the first time.

"Now I know you are almost comfortable, BUT, I need, actually, you need, to pick up all you wish to keep and we're gonna take 10 giant steps backwards," Monck said. "There's a reason for this! When more guests arrive, they will literally push you up against the front of the stage and you'll spend three days with your nose pressed against an eight-foot tall sheet of plywood. "SO, here we go: ONE...great...TWO...wow...THREE...superb, you got it!... FOUR...you're the opening act, people!"

The multitude moves. The collective actually takes direction. "We finally get to 10 and there was a wave of applause for our First Act of peaceful friendly communalism," Monck says. "That's when I realized that maybe being host wouldn't be so hard. I quickly realized, oops, not so fast, wait awhile. I couldn't stop my knees from knocking together."

Before the First Act, however, there was an entirely different show going on.

Famed rock producer Phil Graham had a lot to do with the success of Woodstock in an unofficial capacity.

Photo by Bettmann/Getty Images

"We had only 21 days to build a city once we were kicked out of Wallkill, 18 of which it rained," John Morris says. "That made it even more miraculous, even with a crew of three or four hundred young guys and gals who really cared about building everything in lousy weather, staying in tacky motels, making it happen. I doubt it could ever happen again."

Morris booked most of the bands because that was his job running the Fillmore East for Bill Graham. He had already dealt with most of the agents and managers, one of whom, Bill Belmont, Country Joe McDonald's manager, he brought in as well. "Mike Lang did the rest of the booking for the bands he personally wanted," says Morris, "but Bill and I were the professionals in the room."

John Morris booked most of the bands at Woodstock, a job he performed at Fillmore East for Bill Graham.

One of the managers Morris had to deal with extensively was Jimi Hendrix's guy, Mike Jeffries. "Jeffries was tremendously cooperative," Morris remembers. "We had Jimi going around in circles all day Saturday and Sunday about coming in or not. Mike was a true gentleman. He was holding Jimi off on our say-so. We worked it out that Jimi would end the show. Once the show started, there was never any argument about money with any of the bands."

Except for Iron Butterfly.

"Of course, there was the Iron Butterfly flap. I sent them a telegram that if you read the first letter of each sentence vertically, it read 'fuck you'—this was in response to their ridiculous rock star demands of being taken stage side at an exact time and out the minute their set ended—and I never heard from them again. They were a one-hit wonder anyway. The lady at Western Union was very nice and worked with me on it. I was rather proud of it. I think I still have a copy of it around somewhere."

The Chief Sound Engineer at the Fillmore East, who took over for Bill Hanley, was John Chester. He was 22 when he was sent to the Berkshire Mountains of Massachusetts for a Fillmore-sponsored show, thus he missed the initial phase of the Woodstock set-up. It was Tuesday. He and his crew packed up, drove the equipment back to the Lower East Side of Manhattan and got some much-needed sleep. On Wednesday, they were curious how things were going in Bethel so, with Bob Goddard, he took off for the site on Thursday.

The minute they arrived, Hanley, Langhart and company said, "Oh! Fresh bodies! Have you had any sleep? We certainly haven't!" With that, Chester and Goddard were immediately put to work. "We were just expecting to hang out," says Chester. The first order of business was getting the propane hooked up to the stove so cooking food for the artists could commence. Then Chester found himself on the plumbing detail, supervising a team that went around installing water fountains. After that, he became a general trouble-shooter, getting sand out of water filters, moving the

Image courtesy Michael Stern

An Aquarian Exposition STAFF PASS

NAME ....

SS

Image courtesy Michael Stern

Vehicle Parking Permit

PRODUCTION

JOHN MORRIS

Woodstock organizers quickly found a new site after Wallkill, New York, decided against hosting the event (right). Parking Permits and Staff Passes were issued (above), but with clogged roads and free admission they were mostly worthless.

hospital tent (in the middle of the night) and investigating electrical problems (plentiful because of rain).

Bob Goddard: "It was my responsibility to babysit Joan Baez. Chester and I went up together as visitors, not to work. First thing we did, though, was some plumbing. John went off to play with Bill Hanley on some sound stuff and I went off to do some minor electrical work and help Josh White with the light show. I was in the recording truck 'til the bitter end. Hendrix was wailing right above me but I was still underneath the stage with

TO INSURE THREE DAYS OF PEACE & MUSIC WE'VE LEFT WALLKILL AND ARE NOW AT WHITE LAKE, N.Y.*

Certain people of Wallkill decided to try to run us out of town before we even got there.

They were afraid.

Of what, we don't know. We're not even sure that they know.

But anyway, to avoid a hassle, we moved our festival site to White Lake, Town of Bethel (Sullivan County), N.Y. We could have stayed, but we decided we'd rather switch now, and fight Wallkill later.

After all, the whole idea of the festival is to bring you three days of peace and music.

Not three days of dirty looks and cold shoulders.

Just one more word about those concerned citizens of Wallkill — They're not going to get away with this. Our lawyers have been instructed to start damage proceedings immediately. In the end, we suspect, those citizens responsible

will really have something to worry about.

Now to something a bit more pleasant.

Our New Site.

It's twice the size of our original site. (Who knows, maybe the people of Wallkill did us a favor?) That means twice as many trees. And twice as much grass. And twice as many acres of land to roam around on.

For those of you who have already purchased tickets, don't worry. Your tickets, even though printed Wallkill, will of course be accepted at our new festival site at White Lake in the Town of Bethel.

We'd also like at this time to thank the people of Bethel for receiving the news of our arrival so enthusiastically.

See you at White Lake, for the first aquarian exposition, Aug. 15, 16, and 17.

*White Lake, Town of Bethel, Sullivan County, N.Y.

WOODSTOCK MUSIC & ART FAIR

Image courtesy Michael Stern

the equipment. I certainly could hear him, though.

"Most of the performers, with a couple of exceptions, came in, did their thing on the stage, turned around, waved bye-bye, and went looking for the next copter to get them the hell out there. Joan Baez was one of those exceptions. She hung around for a considerable length of time, both after and before her set, despite being quite pregnant.

"I had worked with her twice before but I don't think she would've recognized me. Still, we got along great. She was doing a dead-on impersonation of Joe Cocker, vocals and all, and that spastic jerk. She had everyone in stitches.

Joan was so funny, and was obviously having a wonderful time. John Morris was so freaked out and swore she was going to go into labor at any minute. And the last thing he needed was another baby born at Woodstock."

The plan was to have the wonderfully psychedelic and groundbreaking Joshua Light Show at Woodstock. The

Bethel was the last place many concertgoers would see law enforcement, who for the most part left Woodstock Nation alone.

Photo by Pictorial Parade/Hulton Archive/Getty Images

Light Show was a staple of Fillmore East shows. Offering the same experience at Woodstock was going to be amazing. Only it wasn't.

Chris Langhart: "One of the reasons Woodstock didn't have the Joshua Light Show like at the Fillmore East was that Joshua got into a little tiff with one of the stage managers who thought his screen was a liability in heavy winds, at which point the stage manager whipped out his knife and cut a slit into it."

Joshua White: "That's true. Woodstock was very upsetting to me personally. I was so angry but it was youth anger, and I vented it, saying how disappointed I was in the stage work and in [Production Stage Manager] Steve Cohen's design, which I thought was downright incompetent. I didn't care who heard me say it and it got back to Steve, thus precipitating a blow-out argument right on the stage in front of a lot of people. I was not big on diplomacy in those days. Hell, I was up there trying to deal with my own gang who were all a little sour anyway.

"Actually, Steve's idea to cut the screen, although terrible to me at the time, was OK because it was the only practical solution. They tried to hang it at sunset, which is a time when winds come up so the thing was turning into a giant sail, and the stage was beginning to pull because it wasn't anchored properly. It was an 80-foot wide screen and they were supposed to hang it but when they tried to pull it up, it got caught in the wind. So Steve put holes in it. I remember hating that idea at first. Ultimately, though, who cares? It wasn't

Photo by Julie Snow/Michael Ochs Archives/Getty Images

Joshua White (below) revolutionized the concert experience with his psychedelic Joshua Light Show, made famous at Fillmore East (left). Heavy winds, however, scuttled plans for the Light Show at Woodstock.

Photo by Bobby Bank/WireImage/Getty Images

such a big screen anyway and people were so far away.

"We performed the first night. We used the screen with the holes in it. It was fine. It had little effect but I got to see what the light show looked like mixed with video. My real problem that night was that the video people got drunk and started what we call tap-dancing on the switcher. Everybody was so moved by the music that they would start to either tap their feet, clap their hands, or, if they had something in their hands like a follow-spot or a TV camera or a switcher for three TV cameras, they'd start cutting in time to the music which is an awful thing to do because then it just turns the visual into mush. And what we got Friday night was mush. I was constantly going down to these guys and they'd be sitting there drunk and stupid. I just couldn't get them to stop it. Hey, at least I got to see what it looked like in a large context. It really changed how I thought about video projection from that moment on.

"So, yeah, we performed that first night. It was only when we came back that second day, there was no screen. We had covered all of our projectors with tarps Friday, things seemed fine, we went back to the motel, but when we came back the next day, the screen was gone. And I was told that it had blown away. So we took everything down Saturday during the concert, packed up, and left."

Bob Goddard: "There were plenty of things that weren't finished right up to the start of the concert. Hanley, Morris, Monck, Langhart plus [Direc-

> There were plenty of things that weren't finished right up to the start of the concert. Hanley, Morris, Monck, Langhart plus [Director of Operations] Mel Lawrence and [Campground Coordinator/Hog Farm Recruiter] Stanley Goldstein had to deal with the fact that the fences were down, so nobody needed tickets anymore to get in. Also, a lot of the artists did not want to go onstage and be the first one. They'd look out at that audience and go 'holy shit.'
> — BOB GODDARD

tor of Operations] Mel Lawrence and [Campground Coordinator/Hog Farm Recruiter] Stanley Goldstein had to deal with the fact that the fences were down, so nobody needed tickets anymore to get in. Also, a lot of the artists did not want to go onstage and be the first one. They'd look out at that audience and go 'holy shit.' This went on throughout the festival as times totally changed and artists did not get to go on at the times they were originally told. Everyone kept getting pushed back and each artist dealt with it in his or her own way. Some were sanguine about it all. Others, like Tim Hardin and Janis Joplin, heroin addicts both, had a big problem with that."

John Chester: "Then there were artists who, to be perfectly frank, were overly medicated, shall we say. The Grateful Dead were amongst the chief offenders. I don't think they were ever afraid of what was going on, but they experienced some electrical shocks upon attempting to plug in. They also just didn't like having to deal with so many extraneous factors. They're used to a nice predictable, technical set-up, and their set was fraught with unpredictability."

As behind-the-scene photographer at the Fillmore East during its heyday, Amalie Rothschild witnessed some of the greatest scenes in rock history, capturing The Who's premier of Tommy in 1969; John and Yoko's surprise encore to a Frank Zappa concert; the jam between the Allman Brothers, the Grateful Dead and Mick Fleetwood in 1970; Janis Joplin's first performance after signing with CBS Records; Jimi Hendrix's New Years Eve concerts and a host of others. Her Woodstock was less memorable, at least at first.

"My Woodstock experience was very peculiar. I really didn't see it as such a great social phenomenon at the time. I couldn't understand the attention it got in the media afterwards. But I've come to understand in the intervening years that it was, indeed, a very brief and a very special moment in history," Rothschild says. "We still had our ideals intact. Peace, love and music was real. We believed that music and who we were, what we were about, was going to change the world for the better in positive, peaceful and loving ways. This mindset contributed to the fact that the event was, indeed, peaceful, unified spiritually and cooperative."

Joshua White: "We got there Wednesday. We'd been setting up for days. They hadn't finished anything so we had to run the power, finish the platforms and do all of the things that were standard. We had done outdoor shows before with these people, but they were done in safer places like

Veteran's Stadium in Philadelphia. They were at the height of hubris, Chip Monck and Steve Cohen thought they could do anything. There was, in some degree, incompetence because they didn't have someone like Chris Langhart in the mix, at least not in any way that helped me. And because we were very physical, we ended up doing a lot of the work, after they built the basic scaffold. There was a floor but they hadn't built the tables or a cover for it all, all the things that we had specified. They just kept yessing us

Photo by Ralph Ackerman/Getty Images

A young couple enjoy the green grass and high times far from the crush of the crowd near the main stage.

to death. 'It'll be there,' they kept saying, but, of course, it wasn't."

John Chester: "I don't know if Woodstock changed me particularly. It certainly gave me a great story to tell. I still find it amazing they got all that built in two weeks. It was an awful lot to put together in two weeks after eight months of preparation. Langhart was heavily involved in it from the beginning and we were sharing an apartment together at the time in Greenwich Village so he'd call me. The stories started at Wallkill at the venue that failed. Then we heard it was Bethel and, hey, we enjoy doing this kind of stuff so off we went...basically to make the scene. Certainly not to work. But we knew everybody who was working

on it so it was a no-brainer we'd go too. I didn't have to put up with any of the disgruntled townspeople because by the time I got there, they weren't coming anywhere near it."

Joshua White: "If it weren't for John Morris, I might not have even gotten involved. And remember, all the people doing it minus Michael Lang were all people I knew and had worked with. John Morris was always the adult in the room. He booked the acts. He made Woodstock work. He thought it a natural to have the light show and I just went along with it. I didn't meet Michael until way downstream. I remember our first meeting was at a hotel in the pouring rain. He seemed like a fine young man with big ideas. He wound up signing off on the light show but besides the signing of the contract, all further communications were with Chip Monck and Steve Cohen, the guys backstage doing the physical labor. They knew exactly what we needed."

John Chester: "I think it wouldn't have been as memorable had there been perfect weather. Our jobs certainly would've been easier. The thing that still fascinates me from the technical side was how well-organized the staff was and the fact that they had so many different people doing different jobs that needed to be done. They got phone lines in! That was essential back in those days. And it was one big battle in and of itself. They had a purchasing agent running a whole crew of people in charge of buying everything that needed to be bought. They had a drafting department on-site to make drawings of things that needed to be built. It was incredibly well-organized. The results were totally chaotic because there wasn't enough time to get anything done, but the concept of how to do it was pretty damn good.

"Chip Monck really stepped up as host. He's a lighting guy, not

Organized chaos was the norm as crews scrambled to finish work before the festival opened.

a host! And most of his lights never got in the air. There were giant scaffolds in the audience. Two on each side. A follow-spot is a large lighting instrument run by a human operator who can change colors and the size of the spot while aiming it at anything they want. There were three or four of them on each side of the stage. That was, essentially, all the lighting we had because all the stuff that was supposed to be hanging from the stage roof wasn't there because the stage roof wasn't capable of holding it up. The only reason the stage was there at all was because it still had the cranes holding it up. The construction cranes weren't supposed to stay there! But they were trapped. By the time they figured out they should be leaving, they couldn't get out. It's a good thing, too, because there wouldn't have been anything over the stage!"

Using privately owned, little-known back roads through adjoining farms, Joshua White claims he had no problems getting in and out of Woodstock. He had the luxury of getting back to the hotel, eating, showering and even swimming in the hotel pool. But after Friday, he had had it. "I just insisted that we leave very late Friday night and we just drove out," he remembers. "At Woodstock, although there were people who stayed behind to drive the truck, I wanted out. I wasn't a happy camper. In fact, I was quite upset. My art, the thing I had done and devoted myself to for the past four years of my life, was treated poorly. And, being a kid, I had a big ego. I didn't want to be around anymore. It was a disaster. The film romanticizes everything but there could be an hour or an hour and a half between set-ups. That's no good. It was terrible. The film makes it all sequentially mellow. I mean, don't get me wrong, the film was fair, but, by its very nature, it condenses time."

Although disgruntled and feeling somewhat unappreciated, White has an image of Woodstock that remains indelibly etched in his mind. "I remember sitting with Bill Graham for hours on the apex looking out at the hundreds of thousands of white people wearing denim and realizing how spectacular an event it turned out to be. All we saw was white skin and denim! We weren't exactly deep pals but we were friendly enough. He felt then and there that what he was doing at the Fillmore was going to come to an end. He knew immediately that the future would be in bigger venues and I believe he came to that conclusion while we sat together [Graham closed the Fillmore East in June of '71]. I felt the same thing. I learned a great deal from him. His wisdom became my wisdom."

Graham knew Woodstock would be a logistical nightmare from the get-go. "It was obvious to me," he said in his book, "that they were rank amateurs who were in way over their heads. ...What came out at Woodstock was that they expected the audience to accept whatever shortcomings they had. Oops. I'm sorry. Ooops, sorry. Sorry, sorry, sorry. It was sloppy in the sense of time. Half hour and 45 minutes between sets? If one guy in a band was late, they

It was obvious to me that they were rank amateurs who were in way over their heads. ...What came out at Woodstock was that they expected the audience to accept whatever shortcomings they had. Oops. I'm sorry. Ooops, sorry. Sorry, sorry, sorry. It was sloppy in the sense of time. Half hour and 45 minutes between sets? If one guy in a band was late, they had to wait for him. Hundreds of thousands of kids pitched their tent... so what were they blessed with? The experience of breathing the same air? They had come from someplace and paid good money to get there and then what did they get?

— BILL GRAHAM

had to wait for him. Hundreds of thousands of kids pitched their tent...so what were they blessed with? The experience of breathing the same air? They had come from someplace and paid good money to get there and then what did they get?"

The first stirrings from the stage, after an interminable wait, most likely came from our convivial co-host, Chip Monck, who, along with John Morris and Wavy Gravy, provided a semblance of reassuring reality to a most unreal situation. When Chip Monck spoke at Woodstock, we stopped whatever we were doing,

Photo by Three Lions/Getty Images

People used any means possible to make it to Woodstock, as these two young men riding in the trunk of a car illustrate.

whatever arguments ensued, whatever drugs we were in the process of consuming, and LISTENED. He wasn't hired for such. He was a lighting guy. But, man, he slipped into that role as if he was born for it.

One of those artists backstage being asked to please go on first was New York City singer/songwriter Richie Havens [1941-2013]. As fate would have it, 15 years after Woodstock, in 1984, I found myself in the position of being his publicist. It was his idea that we both go on the "Doctor Judith Kuriansky Show," broadcast over WABC-AM Radio, as artist and fan who could bring separate remembrances of the event to the New York City airwaves on its 15th Anniversary of Woodstock. I agreed and booked the live radio interview. It was heard once that morning and never again. Luckily, my mom taped it.

"We had been seven miles away at a hotel with all the other entertainers waiting for the cars to drive us to the site," remembered Havens that 1984 morning on the radio, "but we couldn't get there. It was all blocked up. The New York State Thruway was closed, as Arlo [Guthrie] so famously said. That's why there was a seven-hour delay at the start of the show. That one little one-lane road was the only way in. And it was also backed up with cars sitting there for hours and hours not moving. Not one car could get any of the artists to the field where the stage was. It was impossible, and impassable. There wasn't going to be any concert if the artists couldn't show up.

"As I opened up my Holiday Inn window, I saw the first helicopter. It landed right in the driveway of the hotel. They decided then that because we had less equipment, we'd get flown in first. It was my guitarist, my conga drummer and myself, packed to the gills with equipment in this tiny helicopter. I was originally slated to be the fifth performer. But because of extenuating circumstances, I was tabbed to go on first to people who had waited seven hours with no music. There were a whole host of artists milling around backstage who refused to go on first! It took guts. Michael Lang had come up to me and asked me to be first and I said, 'Michael, Jesus, do you want

them to throw beer cans at me? Okay, but if they do, I'm gonna get you for this.' So I did him a favor.

"When I went on the stage, I found a crowd really enthusiastic to see anything at all happening on stage. Even feeling as I was feeling, which was a little bit of being in a strange position, I felt the vibe."

Hunched over his guitar, his caftan shirt already soaked with sweat, Havens didn't get very far before his violently rhythmic strumming broke a string. No problem. He gazed out into the sea of humanity and talked to them as if he was addressing a few friends in his living room. "It's a beautiful day to be all here," he said, "and I'm so glad to be here with you all today because I think we're finding out a little something about ourselves. A hundred million songs are going to be sung tonight. All of them are going to be singing about the same thing, which I hope everybody who came, came to hear, really. And its all about you, actually, and me and everyone around the stage and everyone that hasn't gotten here, and the people all over the world who are gonna read about you tomorrow. Yes! And how really groovy you were, if you dig where that's really at."

Then he went on to perform the first—and one of most iconic—of all the Woodstock performances.

"It was quite an experience for me," he admitted 15 years later on the radio. "My generation had found ourselves at odds with the system. Young people sought new ideas and new ways to express themselves. But the establishment stacked the odds against us. Woodstock was our confirmation. We became brothers but even that term 'brothers' obscures the depth of what really happened. The fact is, something magical happened there and the people who experienced it kept a part of it alive within themselves for the rest of their lives. We were never the same.

"It wasn't a great situation, but the thing was, music got us there, and as long as the music could be focused on, the other negatives were diminished. There was a real sense of belonging together, and recognition of the fact that there were that many of us around. The need to be part of something was paramount and, even today, nothing's changed. We're all still at Woodstock."

Barry Hauser was 16 when he set out on the road with his friend Howie Cohen driving Mrs. Cohen's convertible. Spring Valley was only an hour away. They had seen the ad for the festival in *Rolling Stone* magazine. The fact that their favorite band, The Who, would be there sealed the deal. Howie picked Barry up and they were on-site by 8:00 Friday morning, pitching their little pup tent and exploring the area. Soon, they brought their blanket stage-side and set up shop, away from the tent. Hearing announcements that the music would be late, they decided to nap. Three hours later, they woke up and looked around. The hundreds of people had turned into thousands, then tens of thousands, then hundreds of thousands. They couldn't believe it! "I couldn't even see the end of the people," Barry says. They had never heard of Richie Havens but loved him, wondering why he just kept playing and playing for what seemed like hours. "By the end of his set, we were fans for life."

The set that Richie Havens performed, capped off by his totally improvised "Freedom," was a rousing, uplifting and seminal early moment of the weekend. Watching mesmerized as he physically attacked his guitar, rhythmically stirring up a boil, sweat popping out of his head, beads jangling, caftan swirling, this was freedom, and the ovation he received after playing everything he knew was a testament not only to his courage but to Havens' inner fortitude. We in the Woodstock Nation have loved this man ever since. And he's never disappointed. When Havens announced his retirement after 45 years on the road in 2012, due to complications from a 2010 kidney surgery, we knew the end was near. Havens died at his home in Jersey City, New Jersey, on April 22, 2013, at the age of 72. After he was cremated, his ashes were dropped from the air over the site of the festival on August 18, 2013.

CHAPTER THREE

AS FREE AS BIRDS

inger-songwriter-guitarist Willie Nile was 20 when he had to get from his Buffalo home where he attended the University to his older brother Richard's wedding the weekend of Woodstock in nearby Newburgh, New York. "Summertime, man," he recalls. "I was still reeling a year after my hero, Bobby Kennedy, was killed. My girlfriend at the time, Margaret, would hitchhike with me from Buffalo to New York City all the time in '65, '66. We'd sleep in the park for a few days, check out the music scene, and hitch home.

"We didn't hitch this time. We got a ride with a fella named John Gorman, a close friend of Richard's who was also going to the wedding. He was in graduate school studying law and drove an old yellow Mercedes convertible.

Spread out before the multitude was Woodstock, an event of unimaginable possibilities, sights and sounds.

Image courtesy Michel Stern

John's close friend was Elaine Moynihan, the daughter of Senator Daniel Moynihan. It was, in fact, the Senator's old car. We made our way across New York State having a merry old time. It was great fun. We felt free as birds.

"John said, 'hey, I hear there's this music festival with The Who about an hour away from where we're going! Wanna go?' Did I wanna go? I was a huge Who fan, having already seen them. Then when he said Hendrix would also be there, I said, 'hell yeah, let's go!' We started hearing the radio reports about it as we drove closer. It was Friday.

"At some point, we started slowing down and noticed so many abandoned vehicles on the side of the roads including busses and vans. Tents were pitched too. People started giving us the thumbs-up, probably because of the car itself. There were all sorts of characters walking too. It seemed

Photo by Clayton Call/Redferns/Getty Images

In the great collective, everything was shared: food, drink and, most importantly, a good time.

to be every bit the renaissance festival you'd hope it would be. I swear, right there, on the side of the road, as we crawled forth, were people tending small fires, cooking, washing clothes, jugglers, mimes, street people, hippies, yippies, beatniks, rockers, lost poets and minstrels. We drove the car as far as we could go and joined this community. It had unfolded before us in such a graceful way. We didn't know what to expect. We had no tickets. Hell, we were impoverished college students."

The three of them blended right in as they left the car on the side of the road and started walking. "There were bearded longhairs everywhere plus females and little kids walking around naked.

"The people we encountered were so friendly. The vibe was friendly. We felt welcome. It was a nice day. The sun was out. It wasn't raining. We made our way into the woods and noticed Christmas lights strung through the trees showing us the way to the concert. We started to feel a definite sense of excitement at this point. The woods wound up opening into this huge field with tens of thousands of people and it was like, 'whoa!' There were no fences and we walked straight into this absolutely breathtaking sight that we became part of.

"Now we're wading into the people toward the stage, gently brushing up against all the humanity. The three of us brought two sleeping bags and I had some apples and bananas in my backpack. Plus, we had water. We found a good spot dead center in the back of the front, so to speak. Maybe a few hundred people back, that's it. Right in time for Richie Havens. We sat down, smoked some weed that was passed our way, and a lot of cigarettes. Everybody was so neighborly. We knew we had stumbled upon something really special. To see it, feel it, experience it, right there in front of you, man, the way people treated each other was so inspiring. Everybody was so kind to us.

We were even offered sandwiches. So peaceful. Nobody was rowdy. And we stayed right there in that exact spot all night until about noon the next day. We were just so happy to be there.

"Richie Havens was spectacular. Years later, Richie recorded my song, 'On The Road To Calvary.' It was a great honor for me personally. He was such a beauti-

Fans sit perched on a bus on the festival grounds, soaking up the sun and taking in the view.

ful guy, and a great musician. He lit the fuse, y'know?"

Princeton New Jersey attorney Scott Stoner was 19 in '69 and, along with six other friends in two cars, were just starting out on the road to enlightenment... and Woodstock. "We were going to go to the Atlantic City Pop Festival two weeks earlier but decided Woodstock had the better bands. We were all dedicated followers of rock 'n' roll and despite my over-protective mom trying to convince me that it would be a total disaster, I went anyway. Hell, I had been at Yale for a year and already had a degree in independence. The news reports that started emanating from the area made it sound rather dangerous and the dire warnings just got worse as the festival got started."

They left from New Jersey early Friday morning. Traffic was fine until both cars got to Route 17B when "we hit the traffic jam of all traffic jams." After not moving an inch for over two hours, Scott got out of the car and started walking in the direction that all the cars were facing. "I met some great folks. Some were sitting on the roadside playing guitars. Most were just waiting patiently."

Scott was surprised when traffic started moving again and even more surprised when his own car and the other car they came in drove right past him as his friends waved to him, laughing hysterically. He numbly waved back. "I couldn't believe it," he says, "they just left me there." That's when he realized they weren't coming back. Scott started running down the road. "I saw them turn off into a field to the right but by the time I got there, there was such a sea of

Festivalgoers came in all shapes, sizes and dress.

cars that I couldn't find them. Hell, they had my ticket, my clothes, whatever food I brought, my canteen filled with water, but there didn't seem to be any way to hook up with them so I kept walking to what I assumed was the festival site making a lot of new friends along the way. That's when I realized tickets weren't going to be a necessity. People were swarming in from every imaginable side. There didn't seem to be any real security.

"I went back to the start of the road that led from the highway to the site and encountered a school bus. There were my six buddies laughing like crazy from inside the bus beckoning me on. They had the whole bus yelling, 'hey Scott, hey Scott.' So I embarked and we were driven to the site and there we were! We found a place to put our blankets a little bit to the left of the stage around 1:00 in the afternoon on Friday. It was a good spot. I even met a girl. She was really nice and we wound up spending a few hours together. Then her mother, younger sister and boyfriend showed up. They didn't like the scene and were going to leave. That wasn't unusual. I think a lot of people got there and bailed on the scene when they realized how mammoth it was. Too many people! Ironic that what I thought was totally awesome was actually a deterrent for some. The girl I had been chatting with, I found out later, was only 15. Her mom was really flipping out at this point and they left before the music even started."

Photographer Amalie Rothschild: "When we were living it, it didn't seem special because it just seemed so normal and how it should be and how it will always be. How we all related to each other was real and appropriate and good. Of course, the big thing, which we also couldn't possibly have realized living through it, was that that weekend proved pivotal in the music industry. It was an age when recognition by the promoters that the music was powerful enough to bring so many people together would manifest itself in a new era of exploitation into larger venues and sports stadiums. It was the demise of the small venues. It led to Bill Graham's decision to close both Fillmores. It's business."

Concertgoer Jacob Cohen: "We barely endured Saturday and left early Sunday morning, totally frustrated. The closest we ever got to the stage was a mile away. I clearly remember the main stage and the field in front of the stage. The field seemed to be about a quarter-mile long before it rose up into a big hill with a sea of people all over the place. Weather-wise and comfort-wise, the whole thing was a total disaster for us. (My friend) Saul lost his wire-rim glasses. He had to have them. At one point, we were sitting on the grass. He put his glasses down. The next minute, he couldn't find them. It took us two hours but I found them. That's what I remember most about Woodstock. Finding his glasses.

"When we got home, we ran into friends and that's when we learned for

We barely endured Saturday and left early Sunday morning, totally frustrated. The closest we ever got to the stage was a mile away. I clearly remember the main stage and the field in front of the stage. The field seemed to be about a quarter-mile long before it rose up into a big hill with a sea of people all over the place. Weather-wise and comfort-wise, the whole thing was a total disaster for us. (My friend) Saul lost his wire-rim glasses. He had to have them. At one point, we were sitting on the grass. He put his glasses down. The next minute, he couldn't find them. It took us two hours but I found them. That's what I remember most about Woodstock. Finding his glasses.

— JACOB COHEN

MY BELOVED BROTHERS AND SISTERS: I AM OVERWHELMED WITH JOY TO SEE THE ENTIRE YOUTH OF AMERICA GATHERED HERE IN THE NAME OF THE FINE ART OF MUSIC. IN FACT, THROUGH THE MUSIC, WE CAN WORK WONDERS. MUSIC IS A CELESTIAL SOUND AND IT IS THE SOUND THAT CONTROLS THE WHOLE UNIVERSE, NOT ATOMIC VIBRATIONS. SOUND ENERGY, SOUND POWER, IS MUCH, MUCH GREATER THAN ANY OTHER POWER IN THIS WORLD.

— Swami Satchidinanda in his opening address at Woodstock

Photo by Elliott Landy/Getty Images

An overhead view of the sprawling, 600 acres of Max Yasgur's farm used for the festival.

the first time about all the news reports. We had no idea. It just wasn't very pleasant for us. We were totally unprepared. Like everything else we did at that time, it was all pure reaction. No forethought whatsoever. In the car. Go. That's how we lived our lives back then. We were 16 so what did we know anyway?"

I awoke Friday morning—after falling asleep on the ground—to a swift kick to my side. "I'm sorry, man. Do you want

a toke?" There seemed to be a few hundred people in our little patch of land that had only about a dozen on Thursday night. I accepted the early-morning toke with gratitude, being told it was some fine Columbian weed. I inhaled, let a plume of smoke escape into the face of another new neighbor who didn't seem to mind. Everybody was so tightly packed together! I had left Newark wanting to meet fellow travelers on the road to enlightenment, and now they were practically sitting in my lap. I groggily got up, stretched and turned around behind me. Neil was still sleeping.

My jaw dropped.

There, for as far as the eye could see, leading to that large hill where we hitched down to our present location, was a vista of humanity, so much so

I thought for a moment it was a dream. I never saw so many people in one place at one time and we were at the head of the whole shebang, right by the stage. There were people sitting on a far-off hill who couldn't possibly see the musicians. I gasped, sputtered, stuttered, stammered, and let out the obligatory "oh wow." I looked down to the guy who had shared his weed with me. He was sitting cross-legged with a beatific smile on his face. He knew exactly what I was experiencing. He had experienced the same thing moments earlier. He looked up at me.

"Far out, man."

"Neil! Neil," I screamed. "Look at this!" Neil got up, turned around and whispered, "holy shit." It must have been around 6:00 in the morning. All talk about leaving our amazing spot ceased right then and there. Our neighbors had come more than equipped and they shared fresh fruit, juice, bread and plenty more tokes so that I'd be in the proper frame of mind when the music started at 10:00 that morning (that's what we were led to believe).

By noon, the music was still five hours away but we didn't know that. And we didn't care. We were rocking to our own inner beat as we played more Monopoly, ate more bread and had more tokes. Neil remained steadfastly straight. The sun was making everything hot—really, really hot—so we all took off our tops—boys and girls included—and truly started to get to know our neighbors. Stoned-out conversation, giggles, flirts, arguing about politics and Dylan, laugh-

A cameraman (bottom, right) films singer Nancy Nevins and cellist August Burns of Sweetwater as they perform Friday night.

Photo by Archive Photos/Getty Images

ter, more flirting, toking, sipping warm sweet red wine, getting baked under the hot sun and getting totally baked on weed. A double baking! No one worried about sunburn. Despite still no music—we all had our half-baked theories about that—it was one of the more pastoral, communal, sweetly happy times of the whole weekend. It was so much fun, and I was right where I wanted to be, that I didn't care if the music ever started.

What we couldn't possibly have known at the time was the fact that the bands scheduled to play on Friday couldn't get in as all roads leading in and out of the festival site were bumper-to-bumper stopped dead for hours on end and the helicopter system had yet to start. Once we saw the copters, we thought the show was imminent. We were wrong. By 4:00 we were yelling for music. Loud. It was still an hour away. Some folks started throwing stuff at the stage. The mood had changed. What we also didn't know was that none of the artists in the backstage area wanted to go on as they were afraid of us. They had good reason to be.

Co-promoter John Morris stepped up to the microphone to make an announcement. I was eating a cheese sandwich someone had given me when he said…"Many people have come here today, many, many more than we knew, dreamed or even thought would be possible. We're gonna need each other to help each other and work this out because we're taxing the system that we've set up. We're gonna be bringing the food in. But it's a free concert from now on. That doesn't mean that anything goes. What that means is we're going to put the music up here for free. What it means is that the people who are backing this thing, who put up the money, are going to take a bit of a bath. A big bath. That's no hype, that's true, they're going to get hurt. What it means is that these people have it in their heads that your welfare is a hell of a lot more important…than the dollar. Now, the one major thing that you have to remember tonight, when you go back up to the woods to go to sleep or if you stay here, is that the man next to you is your brother. And you damn well better treat each other that way because if you don't, then we blow the whole thing…"

"Well, it was meant to calm nerves, communicate the fact that we had things under control and that everything was fine," Morris says. "The truth was that I was hardly sure of any of those things. There were SO many people in that field. We hadn't collected the tickets. We couldn't get anybody in or out. We were sort of frozen. I just figured that what we had to do is set a 'let's work together' tone and make this happen. I was trying to impress upon people that this was not a disaster. We're going to make it work. We'll get the acts up here somehow, make you happy, and make us happy. That was, basically, what I was thinking when I made that statement.

"There's a scene in the film where a Friday morning huddle takes place with Michael, Artie (Kornfeld), two or three others and myself. Artie is saying 'we have no money. We have to collect the money. Let's do like the Catholic Church and send girls out in diaphanous gowns with collection baskets and ask for money.'

"I looked at Artie and told him, 'I'm an ex-Catholic. That never happened and, frankly, it's a ridiculous idea.' You can see me walking away from the group while throwing my hands up in the air. I then went to my office, picked up the phone, called John (Roberts) and Joel (Rosenman), and said, 'look, I think we need to set a tone here. We've got more people than we can handle right in front of us and we have to figure out a way to handle them. No way are we going to ask them for money. We have to just carry on with the concert. My suggestion is that I go onstage and declare it a free concert. I think that will cement a relationship with the audience that, hey, we're givin' it to you so you help us. Let's make it work."

Once again, as he was throughout the weekend, John Morris was right.

Hugh Romney also stepped up to the microphone. He had been feeding kids, helping those too stoned-out to deal with the enormity of the situation, and, generally, just being a calming presence. This is the man who became known as Wavy Gravy and donned a clown costume for most of his career because, as Jerry Lewis taught us, there is honor in being the clown. "The brown acid isn't poison," he said, "just poorly manufactured, so just take half a hit!" His people brought in 1,500 pounds of rolled oats, 1,500 pounds of

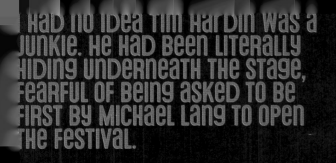

I HAD NO IDEA TIM HARDIN WAS A JUNKIE. HE HAD BEEN LITERALLY HIDING UNDERNEATH THE STAGE, FEARFUL OF BEING ASKED TO BE FIRST BY MICHAEL LANG TO OPEN THE FESTIVAL.

bulgur wheat, soy sauce, apricots, almonds, wheat germ, pots and pans, plastic knives, forks and spoons plus 160,000 paper plates.

As the first band to perform, Sweetwater's set was used as a de facto sound check. Lead singer Nancy Nevins was the first woman to grace the stage. Regrettably, their set was totally underwhelming, and I took off in search of the hot dog stands that were still operating on Friday.

I had never heard of Bert Sommer but when he delicately finger-picked his way through Paul Simon's "America," leaving some important lines out of the song, but crystallizing Simon's intent in the process, I realized Simon was writing about us. Sommer's fragile delivery, like wisps of cigarette smoke, evaporated into the hot summer air. He seemed to be barely holding it together. The result, though, was spellbinding and I wondered how the people in the back could even hear him. They certainly couldn't see the strain on his face. I fell in love with the guy right there and then. "Counting

A talented artist, Tim Hardin's extreme stage fright and heroin addiction made him an unreliable

Photo by Archive Photos/Getty Images

the cars on the New Jersey Turnpike/ They've all come to look for America." The America we thought we knew was being hijacked...and only here, with all my new friends, could America rebound. At least that's what we were naïve enough to think.

Tim Hardin was one of the folk artists I had been looking most forward to seeing due to his exquisite compositions "The Lady Came From Baltimore" and "Reason To Believe." Bobby Darin had covered his brilliant "If I Were A

Photo by Michael Ochs Archives/Getty Images

Only moments before the start of the festival, Chip Monck was coaxed into serving as Woodstock emcee.

Carpenter" and Hardin returned the favor by covering Darin's protest song "Simple Song Of Freedom" (as good a protest song as anything Dylan ever wrote). Hardin seemed so cool. He played the blues and you could tell he felt the blues deep down in his soul. So many artists—including Rod Stewart, Joan Baez, Johnny Cash, Robert Plant, The Four Tops, Neil Young and The Carpenters—have recorded his songs.

The man, though, was simply in no shape to perform. When he finally went on, his set was, in a word, awful. His timing was off, his voice faltered. He was the first big musical disappointment of Woodstock (there would be more).

Nineteen-year old Barry Schneier was in the audience that night. He remembers Hardin's set differently. "It was a real hoot when Tim Hardin played and I looked up and saw a guy I knew, Gilles Malkine, playing guitar with him! He was from Woodstock, and I had met him there those few times when I visited friends. We got to know each other. I hadn't seen him in a while but was knocked out to see him performing on the huge Woodstock stage with Tim Hardin. I couldn't quite believe it! There came a point in one song when he was facing Hardin. At first, I thought they were jamming together on their guitars, but then I realized Gilles was talking to him. I asked Gilles about that later, and he told me that he was desperately trying to keep Tim Hardin from totally losing it onstage. He was that [messed] up."

Hardin would go on to overdose on heroin in Los Angeles at the age of 39 in 1980. It hit home hard, as if a precious piece of my past died right along with him.

I made my way around the perimeter—while Neil held our spot—to meet people who I instantly loved. I know, corny, right? I knew Neil was sitting there alone but he really wasn't alone, was he? And I was in the business of making new friends, talking politics, boasting about the Miracle Mets (who would go on to win the '69 World Series after being the worst team in the history of baseball in '62).

I got back just in time for Ravi Shankar and his sound sent me into the stratosphere. I never heard someone play sitar right in front of me and I became immediately demonstrative. That's when a dude to my left leaned over and said in my ear, "relax, he's just tuning up." We were upset when he stopped his set short because of a few raindrops that weren't bothering anybody...except him, I guess.

With the rain still drizzling, singer-songwriter Melanie won our hearts as she sat on a chair with her acoustic guitar all by herself. She was only 22. I could see how scared she was. And how beautiful. When it started to rain a little heavier during her set, Chip Monck presciently took the microphone between

Friday's headliner Joan Baez sang to a mostly sleeping village, ending her set and a long day of music with "We Shall Overcome."

songs to gently tell everyone that if they all lit candles, it would help to keep the rain away. They did but it didn't. People came with candles? What it did do, though, was present a vista of unbelievable humanity in the dark of night as the whole village seemingly lit up in the form of tens of thousands of little lights. Looking at it from the stage, Melanie was awestruck. She later wrote about it in "Lay Down (Candles In The Rain)." The practice took hold in other concerts, in other years, first with lighters and today with cell phones.

Then came Arlo.

Arlo Guthrie had been waiting and waiting backstage not knowing when he was going on (like all the other acts) . He spent his time imbibing in whatever substances were floating around backstage. By the time he was called to the stage, he was wasted, stoned to the bone, feeling no pain, and spontaneaously coming up with one of the most famous lines of the weekend.

"Yeah! It's far-out, man! I don't know, like how many of you can dig how many people there are, man. I was rapping to the fuzz, right? Can you dig it? Man, there's supposed to be a million and a half people here by tonight! Can you dig that? The New York State Thruway's closed, man! Yeah, a lotta freaks!"

He made himself laugh. Us too. That's when we first understood the fact that the whole world was watching.

The Friday headliner, Joan Baez, barefoot and pregnant, didn't look scared at all. In fact, she looked downright brazen and she made the most of her pulpit by preaching to the choir, telling us about her husband, David Harris, imprisoned for draft evasion, something we all had to think about doing. It gave her set an extra gravitas, especially when she sang "I Dreamed I Saw Joe Hill Last Night."

Joe Hill [1879-1915] was a Swedish immigrant who wrote songs that propelled the labor movement in this country. He joined the International Workers of the World (IWW), but since he changed people's hearts and minds to the left, he was framed for murder by right-wing anti-union forces and put to death via firing squad at the age of 36 on the trumped-up charges, thus becoming a martyr for the cause of workers' rights. It is said his last statement was "don't mourn, organize!" It was her husband's favorite song and it almost made me cry when Joan Baez sang it close to 2:00 in the morning.

She sang it to the mostly sleeping village in front of her. She was the queen and when she ended her set with "We Shall Overcome," a sense that everything, after all, was going to be alright, hung in the air like sweet incense. She calmed our frazzled nerves.

When silence finally ensued, at the end of that long day, I didn't know what to do with myself. I was too fraught with emotion. I needed to talk things out. There was this girl, silently weeping at the injustice of it all. I made my way over to her and we talked until almost 4:00 in the morning. Then we kissed and said goodbye.

Photo by Ralph Ackerman/Getty Images

India's most famous musician, Ravi Shankar captivated and amazed the Woodstock audience, many who had never heard or witnessed anything like his performance.

Photo by Ralph Ackerman/Getty Images

CHAPTER FOUR

BUT MOM, THERE WILL BE ADULT SUPERVISION

Neil Yeager was 16 when he suggested we go to Woodstock.

We were sitting in the back room of Concord Insurance Company in Newark trapped in our meaningless jobs of filing cancelled policies while on the radio the ad kept coming on with a list of the bands.

"Man, we should go to that! It's unbelievable. Listen to that list of bands!"

"I suggested it but I didn't really think we were going to go," remembers Neil.

I wound up making the decision and the only thing Neil could think to ask was, "what do we bring?"

"Nobody knew how to go to festivals," he says today. "Nobody knew what a festival was! We certainly didn't. We had no idea what we were getting ourselves into. I remember going home and telling my mom that I was going to this music and art fair in Upstate New York to which my mom said, 'no you're not.'

There was a lot to be discovered at Woodstock, but adult supervision was nowhere in sight.

"But there will be adult supervision!"

Then Neil promised his mother he would call from Woodstock to let her know he was safe. And that was it. I picked Neil up at his house and off we went having no idea what we were getting ourselves into.

"We weren't alone," agrees Neil. "Nobody knew. Obviously, Woodstock became iconic but it wasn't so at the time. The *Times* headline said 'Traffic Uptight At Hippie Fest.' I was surprised it even made the newspapers. That's the first point where I realized it was a big deal. While we were in it, though, it was kind of surreal as it was unfolding. We didn't know Woodstock was to be such a brazen interpretation of a coming-to-gether culture. For us it was just a bunch of kids.

"It would be a very big deal to just see one of these artists on television," Neil says. "We had no access to artists except on their records. More than most people, we had been going to Asbury Park Convention Hall down the Jersey shore or the Fillmore East in New York City. It would be a thrill to just see one artist.

"The enormity of having all this great talent, all these people who we idolized, in one place, one after another, was intoxicating in a way you couldn't imagine.

Photo courtesy Michael Stern

With the whole world watching, Woodstock Nation was on its best bohemian behavior – even picking up garbage when asked.

Photo courtesy Michael Stern

"I still can't quite believe it. I remember looking at all the naked people in the pond, too. That just didn't happen in our lives! I mean, hell, we weren't real hippies. We lived with our parents. We were weekend hippies. Fashion hippies. But all of a sudden, we were in it. And it all became real. Not watching on TV, or listening on radio, or reading about in a newspaper, or seeing it in a movie, we were inside of it. And it was happening all around us. I don't think we knew its ramifications as we walked around but it sunk in when I called my mom. Then, once we realized, that sense of 'the whole world's watching' was very prevalent. We knew at that point that this was not just some concert we were at like we had been to so many times before."

We had slept right where we grooved to the Friday lineup. In fact, there were tens of thousands of us just sleeping right there until the next day. We had no sleeping bags, no tent, no towel, we just slept on the damp ground. We never left.

Chief of Operations Mel Lawrence was the first person to talk to us early Saturday morning: "Why don't we just clean up our areas? We're going to pass along garbage bags for you to put your trash in, and then we'll pick them up." We did as instructed.

MTV certainly didn't exist. There were very primitive channels for accessing talent other than TV shows like 'Hullabaloo,' 'Shindig,' 'Where The Action Is' and 'The Ed Sullivan Show.' And here was just this overload of stardom in one place. How could we not go? Plus, being in a crowd that size was something most people didn't experience either. We were babes in the woods. Like everybody else.

"And we were so in awe knowing we would be seeing all these bands in one place for several days. We brought coffee cakes, Ring Dings, sandwiches, two big canteens of water, pot, a tent, clothing, towels and Monopoly and, of course, left everything in the car for the four days never to return to it.

In the 1960s "The Ed Sullivan Show" was one of the few venues where kids could see their favorite bands, such as The Beatles chatting here with Ed Sullivan.

Photo by Bettman/Getty Images

Max and Miriam Yasgur rented 600 acres of their dairy farm for the festival. Like us, they had no idea just how BIG the moment would be. "Kids were running motorcycles through our fields planted with corn," Miriam Yasgur is quoted in Michael Lang's *Back To The Garden*. "They were breaking cornstalks and Max promptly called Michael and said, 'do you know they're destroying this field, which is not part of the land that I rented to you at all?' It didn't take very long until a whole group of young kids came out and put signs all around the field: 'DON'T RIDE THROUGH THIS FIELD...THESE ARE MAX'S CROPS.'

"Nobody ever rode through the field again. They kept going around it. People were camping along the sides of the road and they started coming up my driveway and I went out and I said to the young people, 'look, we cannot have people camping along the driveway. Our men are working, they have to get in and out.' They moved. Nobody camped on my driveway. Nobody camped near the dairy."

Interviews with police, town board members, farmers and locals all said the same thing: how well behaved we were.

Quill was supposed to be the band to be catapulted to stardom as a direct result of its Woodstock appearance opening Saturday's schedule at 12:15 in the afternoon, a schedule that would be beset with so many delays that the final band that night, Jefferson Airplane,

Photo courtesy Michael Stern

Cars sprawled across the counryside, but when asked people stayed out of Max Yasgur's cornfields.

PERFORMERS SCHEDULE

		On	Off
Gates Open at 1:00 p. m.			
August 15th			
Sweet Water		4:00	4:55
Bert Somers		5:00	5:30
Tim Hardin		5:35	6:30
Richie Havens		6:35	7:30
BREAK		7:30	8:00
Ravi Shanker		8:00	9:30
BREAK		9:30	10:00
Incredible String Band		10:00	11:00
Freddie Neil		11:00	11:15
Arlo Guthrie		11:20	12:00
Joan Baez		12:05	*****
Gates Open at 12:00 p. m.			
August 16th			
Quill		1:30	2:15
Mountain		2:20	3:05
Canned Heat		3:10	4:10
Santana		4:15	5:10
Sly		5:15	6:15
BREAK		6:15	6:45
Keef Hartley		6:50	7:35
Creedence Clearwater		7:40	8:35
Grateful Dead		8:40	9:40
Janis Joplin		9:45	10:45
BREAK		10:45	11:10
The Who		11:15	12:45
Jefferson Airplane		12:50	1:50
Jam		1:50	*****
Gates Open 12 noon			
August 17th			
Iron Butterfly		1:00	2:00
Joe Cocker		2:05	3:05
Johnny Winter		3:10	4:10
Ten Years After		4:15	5:15
BREAK		5:15	5:45
Country Joe & The Fish		5:45	6:45
Crosby, Stills & Nash		6:50	7:50
The Band		7:55	8:55
BREAK		9:00	10:00
Sha-Na-Na		10:00	10:20
Blood, Sweat & Tears		10:30	11:30
Jimi Hendriks		11:35	*****

EMMANUEL DUNAND/AFP/Getty Images

Unimaginable delays made this original Woodstock performers' schedule laughable. A late scratch, Iron Butterfly was booked to play Sunday afternoon.

Photo by Archive Photos/Getty Images

Robin Williamson of The Incredible String Band, a popular psychedelic folk band formed in Scotland.

wouldn't take the stage until 8:00 the next morning. Ultimately, Saturday's lineup—including delays—would encompass a staggering 21 straight hours until the final note at 9:40 a.m. the next day.

Quill's set, though, was boring, and the band didn't make the *Woodstock* movie or the subsequent soundtracks. Instead of riding a wave of publicity from the concert, Quill vanished, their moment of fame long ago forgotten by all but the most ardent rock historians.

Country Joe & the Fish would perform as a band on Sunday, the first band back after the torrential rain, and they were great. Starved for music as we were, as well as being plain starving, we ate up their set. But it was Country Joe McDonald's impromptu solo set Saturday that launched a career for the performer who would emerge as one of the most popular counterculture acts. While Country Joe & the Fish disbanded shortly after Woodstock, the moment not only defined Country Joe's career, it made it possible.

On that fateful Saturday, though, it just happened to be that the band's tour manager Bill Belmont was on the Woodstock production crew. When Santana appeared mired in technical difficulties in preparing for their set after Quill, there was dead time that had John Morris freaking out. Noticing Joe taking in the sights and just naturally grooving to it all, Morris approached Belmont, asking, "is Country Joe ready to start his solo career?" Joe, for his part, was totally enjoying the day, sitting on the stage, basking in the beautiful sunshine and looking out at the vista of humanity spread out before him like a Hieronymus Bosch painting.

"When asked to perform, it really broke my reverie, man," McDonald says. "I thought, 'this is crazy!' It didn't freak me out so much to perform in front of so many people, but I had no guitar. Plus, I hadn't performed alone on stage with a guitar in over three years. I didn't bring one. Somehow, though, one of the stagehands found a really nice cheap Yamaha guitar, an FG-150, and gave it to me but without a strap ... I can't play without a guitar strap!"

You have to be resourceful if you want to be a tour manager. No guitar strap? No problem! Belmont wound up cutting a piece of line from the stage rigging, tied it on to the guitar and handed it to Joe.

"Go!"

And with that, Joe was literally pushed out to the center of the stage where the microphone stood on a mic stand. Moseying on up there as if without a care in the world, he stared blankly at a cross-section of American youth. He had no idea what to sing. He never even thought about it. Sure, he had the set down pat for what would transpire on the following day with his beleaguered band already on the precipice of breaking up, but here he was with a borrowed acoustic guitar and a hastily put-together strap. He paused a moment, thought about it, and proceeded to sing a song he had written about a former love.

Janis

"Into my life on waves of electrical sound/
And flashing light she came/
Into my life with the twist of a dial/
The wave of her hand, the warmth of her smile.

"And even though I know that you and I/
Could never find the kind of love we wanted together/
Alone I find myself missing you and I, you and I.

"It's not very often that something special happens/
And you happen to be that something special for me/
And walking on grass where we rolled and laughed in the moonlight/
I find myself thinking of you and I, you and I, you.

"Into my eye comes visions of patterns/
Designs the image of her I see/
Into my mind the smell of her hair
The sound of her voice, we once were there.

"And even though I know that you and I/
Could never find the kind of love we wanted together/
Alone, I find myself missing you and I, you and I, you."

Whether Janis Joplin heard her former boyfriend's lament is unknown. He might have been thinking about what had happened two days previous, Thursday, when they both arrived at the Holiday Inn at around the same time. It's not something he's ever been quick to talk about.

"I was in Santiago, Chile, with left-wing filmmakers making a movie when I heard she died," he softly says today. "Somebody brought a *Rolling Stone* magazine on the set and showed me the news. I can't say I was surprised. When I was at Woodstock, Janis also got there early. There weren't too many people yet at that Holiday Inn, but she asked me to come into her room. It

was Thursday. We had been broken up since right before Monterey in the spring of '67. I had moved on, got married, had a kid.

"Anyway, she invites me over to her room and we were just hanging around in the room, and then we had a sexual oral encounter that she instigated much to my surprise. Afterwards, she looked quite satisfied with herself. She opens up the drawer right next to the bed, pulls out her works, and starts to get ready to shoot up. I said, 'I'm not watching you do this. You've got to be joking.'

"Janis was so damn schizophrenic. She really did have two distinct per-

Never one to miss a good time, Janis Joplin burned the candle at both ends until, sadly, the fire went out.

Photo by Jim Marshall/courtesy Heritage Auctions

sonalities. When I said that, she flipped into her mean Janis. 'Well man,' she said, 'I did your thing for you. Now you won't even watch me do my thing?'

"'I didn't want what happened here,' I said. "The whole thing was your idea. I refuse to sit here and watch you kill yourself. So...goodbye.'

"That's why when I heard she died, I wasn't surprised. This was in an age when it was so unusual for a woman to have her own thing, her own identity and her own band. I knew the guys in Big Brother [Joplin's band, Big Brother and the Holding Company]. And I knew they'd call her on her shit just like I used to. But I also knew that her new band would not ever be able to call her on her shit. She was so famous by then. I mean, geez, the Southern Comfort people were sending her free cases of Southern Comfort. Everyone was having a good old time watching her die.

"So I might not have been surprised when I got the news in Chile...just sad. I went to a

church and lit a candle at a little altar and said a prayer for her. I knew how lonely she always was. I was alone at the time also and empathized with her.

Janis could be surrounded by people and still feel so alone. She had no peer group. The Beatles had each other. Elvis had his boys. She treated her loneliness by self-medicating with heroin."

Before they broke up, Janis asked Joe to write her a song. "I realized with hindsight that she wanted me to write a song for her to sing, instead of one about her," Joe says. "I was up in Canada one day strumming a chord pattern on my guitar and within 20 minutes had written 'Janis.' I consider it my most beautiful song."

After performing a few country songs to the Woodstock crowd, Country Joe was having trouble figuring out what else to sing. He also noticed something. Nobody was listening. Nobody was paying any attention! "But everyone was happy," he remembers, "like a giant family picnic. I wound up walking offstage because I simply didn't know what to do next. I was talking to Bill [Belmont, his tour manager] in the wings and no one even noticed I had left the stage!

"Do you think it would be okay if I did the cheer?" asked Joe, who was saving it for later to do with the whole band.

"What different does it make? No one's listening to you at all anyway," Belmont said. "Do whatever you want."

Reassured and relaxed, Country Joe walked back out on the stage and yelled "Gimme an F!"

"All of a sudden, everybody stopped talking. They looked at me, and they roared back, 'F!' And then I did the whole fuck cheer followed by 'Fixin'-To-Die Rag.' Interestingly enough, when you're performing outdoors, you can't really hear the audience because the sound goes up. It doesn't bounce around off the walls like in an indoor venue. So I started haranguing them to sing louder 'cause I couldn't really hear them.

"C'mon people! How can you expect to stop the war if you don't sing louder?

Photo by Archive Photos/Getty Images

The audience paid little attention to Country Joe McDonald until he started spelling things out.

I-Feel-Like-I'm-Fixin'-To-Die Rag

"Well, come on all of you big strong men/
Uncle Sam needs your help again/
He's got himself in a terrible jam/
Way down yonder in Vietnam/
So put down your books and pick up a gun/
We're gonna have a whole lotta fun.

"And it's one, two, three, what are we fighting for?/
Don't ask me, I don't give a damn/
Next stop is Vietnam/
And it's five, six, seven, open up the pearly gates/
Well there ain't no time to wonder why/
Whoopee! We're all gonna die.

"Well, come on generals, let's move fast/
Your big chance has come at last/
Now you can go out and get those Reds/
'Cause the only good Commie is one that's dead/
And you know that peace can only be won/
When we've blown 'em all to kingdom come.

"Come on Wall Street, don't be slow/
Why man, this is war au-go-go/
There's plenty good money to be made/
By supplying the Army with the tools of its trade/
But just hope and pray that if they drop the bomb/
They drop it on the Viet Cong.

"Come on mothers throughout the land/
Pack your boys off to Vietnam/
Come on fathers, and don't hesitate/
To send your sons off before it's too late/
And you can be the first ones on your block/
To have your boy come home in a box."

"Then they started standing up, singing, and I finished it, came offstage again, my name is announced again, the cheers are loud, and that, right there, was the launch of my solo career.

"The other thing I didn't know at the time was that the Woodstock film director Michael Wadleigh and the crew he picked had a history of social-political American filmmaking. Michael was onstage pretty much filming all the performers. And he was very politically sympathetic. If it hadn't been him, I seriously doubt the fuck cheer or the rag would've even been included in the movie or its subsequent soundtracks. It was a perfect storm of circumstances. It was like I was born to write that song."

Dropping the F-bomb in public was a big deal in 1969. When he asked us to spell it out, we did. Then he asked us, "What's that spell?" And we told him. Three times he asked us, and three times we screamed it. It was liberating. It was cathartic. It was hilarious. It was thrilling. It was therapeutic and it was wonderful. It was one of the high points of Woodstock weekend, a galvanizing moment-in-time that represented unhinged unmoored FREEDOM—the same freedom that Richie Havens had extemporaneously chanted Friday—freedom from societal, parental, governmental, educational, religious and behavioral restraints. It felt so good. It was a metaphor for everything we felt, believed in and wanted in one all-purpose syllable. And it was Country Joe who let that pony ride free within our souls. (He would go on to do the same thing even more dramatically the following day, thus my claim that it's Country Joe McDonald who was the heart and soul of Woodstock...but more on that later.)

"It was the perfect expletive to describe how we felt as a generation," McDonald says today.
Joe had grown up as what they used to call a "red-diaper baby," born to progressive left-wing politically active parents. He served in the military. He listened over and over to the old scratchy Woody Guthrie 78s of his parents.

"Fixin'-To-Die-Rag" kicked the door down. It was punk before punk existed. ("It certainly wasn't folk music," laughs Joe.) The way he played the guitar, his attitude, the way he presented himself, he was a harbinger of what was to come within youth culture including punk, grunge and even profane gangsta rap. Using what he calls "working-class language," he stormed the barricades of good taste, "because we were expected, as a generation, to politely take what they were giving out to us. And the one thing that the cheer was not is polite. The attitude was brand new. It certainly wasn't anti-soldier. Hell, they sang it in Vietnam while fighting."

The crowd was still buzzing about Santana's 45 minutes of pure adrenaline but nothing followed them except silence and we were getting antsy. That's when I split, leaving Neil alone to man the site. I didn't return until Canned Heat that night. But before them, the affable and lovable John Sebastian, wandering around in a stoned-out haze with a perpetual smile on his face, not advertised, not expecting to play, was asked to perform solo. His band, The Lovin' Spoonful, had broken up and he was just digging the sights and sounds, getting high and high-fiving all his new friends.

But he agreed.

"Thank you! I don't know if you can really tell how amazing you look, but you are, truly, amazing! You're a whole city! I've been out in California and I've been living here in a tent. I had the tent for about four days and met this lady that does tie-dying so she taught me how to do it, and I got sheets and I put them up on the inside of my tent and it's sooooo groovy to come here and see all you people living in tents. A cloth home is all you need if you got love, I tell ya. This is a song about rainbows, I guess."

And with that rambling hello, John Sebastian launched into "Rainbows All Over Your Blues," a song that would grace his 1970 solo debut, *John B. Sebastian*. It's a delightful song, made even more delicious by his good-natured delivery. We ate it up and demanded more.

"Oh boy," he said with a sheepish smile when he came back. "... Wow! Just love everybody all around you and clean a little garbage on the way out and everything's gonna be alright. You're doing so well, man. This is gonna work!"

For a moment in time, The Incredible String Band was one of the coolest acts in the land. Their music was delicate and their sound gentle. But taking the stage early Saturday evening at Woodstock, their mellow nuances were badly out of place. "What a great act to follow," said Canned Heat drummer Fito De La Parra, as the band waited in the wings. Canned Heat's blues-busting antics was like a shot of adrenalin. Its hour-long, high-energy set blew Woodstock Nation away.

Canned Heat was notoriously rowdy. Their trip to and from Woodstock illustrated the point.

"We were totally unrehearsed, and not at our best," Fito says. "I was so exhausted because the night before Woodstock, we played the Fillmore East. I didn't care. I didn't know what Woodstock meant, if anything."

It was best not to poke The Bear, as journalists discovered when meeting Bob Hite of Canned Heat.

Photo by Ed Perlstein/Redferns/Getty Images

"WE'RE GOING TO REPORT THE NEWS, MAN." "NO YOU'RE NOT. WE'RE GOING TO MAKE NEWS. GET OUT OF OUR WAY!"

"I had to physically drag Fito out of bed to go to Woodstock," says manager Skip Taylor. "I barged into his hotel room. He refused to go. Then I turned on the TV and we listened to what everyone was talking about. Good thing I had a duplicate key for his room or he wouldn't have let me in."

The drama continued when the band had to wait four hours at the local airport. They were fuming. Massive singer Bob "The Bear" Hite was not a person to be trifled with. There was a helicopter that was supposed to be for press... until The Bear hijacked it. They saw the copter and its two occupants prior to its takeoff. They ran straight at it.

"Where do you think you're going," Hite snarled.

The rock journalists looked like scrawny teenagers compared to big Bob Hite.

"We're going to report the news, man."

"No you're not. We're going to make news. Get out of our way!"

With that, the 300-pound Hite grabbed the first scribe he could get his hands on, yanked him out of the copter and onto the tarmac, bruising his knees in the process. The other reporter gladly gave up his seat, thus five Canned Heat guys were on their way to Woodstock.

Photo by Tucker Ranson/Pictorial Parade/Hulton

Canned Heat's singer and harmonica player Alan "Blind Owl" Wilson rocks the Woodstock stage Saturday evening.

Sitting on the trunk of a convertible far from the mainstage, a couple takes in the scene from the fringe.

Photo by Ralph Ackerman/Getty Images

"We were rowdier, bigger and badder than they were. They were not going to fight us for the damn copter," cracks Fito.

Up, up and away. It's 3:30 Saturday afternoon. Little do they know they wouldn't hit the stage for another four hours. Their road crew was scrambling to get all their equipment in on time despite all roads being blocked. Canned Heat's road crew had left at approximately 3:00 Saturday morning from Second Avenue in Lower Manhattan, right outside the Fillmore East, and started driving. Twelve hours later Saturday afternoon they were in the vicinity but still not there until fans, locals and a few burly truckers helped them actually move abandoned cars off the road. "We have to get Canned Heat's gear to the stage," they'd yell.

"It was their sacred mission," Fito says. "It's usually two or three hours tops but 12? Next to impossible and impassable, man. But they did it.

"When I looked down at the people from the helicopter, I just went, 'oh wow.' I'll never forget it. And to think I wasn't going to go no matter what. Then we see our truck from the air arriving right next to the stage. I couldn't believe it. How'd they do it? I've always said roadies never get enough credit. Everybody always concentrates on the artists."

Manager Skip Taylor: "Chip Monck came up to us before we even disembarked and asked us when we wanted to go on. There was a band on stage and I asked, 'who's that?' He said, 'that's the Incredible String Band.' I said, 'great! We'll play next.'"

They might have thought that it was

not a great set but, from the crowd, they provided the perfect impetus for us to really get down, dance around and wave our arms in the air like we just didn't care. Freedom. Beauty. Head-banging at its finest. Decades before the metal crowd boasted of the phenomenon of banging one's head, in the movie you can see Canned Heat, in all their ragged glory, doing just that. Then some guy from the crowd leaps onstage and starts dancing with The Bear who you'd think would crack him one across the head, but, instead, puts his arm around him, smiles and continues to sing. The fan then actually reaches into The Bear's front pocket, pulls out his pack of cigarettes, lights one up and starts smoking. It's an amazing moment.

Fito: "Many of the bands had horrible problems getting their equipment to the site. So we do our set, not one of our better sets, I admit, and we wind up stealing a car to get the hell out of there. We were carjackers! It was a rented limo and we, uh, sorta, liberated it, just borrowed it for a few hours. We had to get out of there!

Skip: "There was no other way. It was parked right there. I saw the keys in the ignition. We looked around for the limo driver. I popped the trunk. We put our equipment in, nobody said a word. And we drove off. We didn't know where we were even going but we got about a hundred yards away and there's cars littering the road. The Bear gets out and starts lugging cars to the side of the road so we could get through.

Fito: "Mountain bassist Felix Pappalardi was with us. His band had followed us and they had had just finished. He jumped into the stolen limo with us.

Skip: "We just kept driving until we saw the Holiday Inn. I told the guys to wait while I went up to the front desk. Big Brother & The Holding Company were staying there. I saw their name on the list. And I know damn well that they're never going to get there so I said we were Big Brother & The Holding Company and they led us right upstairs to their rooms. We wound up hiding the limo in the woods.

"We got up the next day, went back to the airport, and I went straight to the Hertz Rent-A-Car counter and gave them the keys to the limo, telling them that somebody is going to be looking for it. But here's the kicker: seven years later, although I know it's hard to believe, we're coming into JFK Airport in New York and have a limo waiting for us. We settle into the limo and told the driver the story, upon which the guy slams on the brakes right on the Long Island Expressway, and he goes, "THAT WAS MY CAR!"

Photo by Archive Photos/Getty Images

While Canned Heat and other bands left Woodstock as soon as they could, the festival crowd stayed for more.

Photo by Ralph Ackerman/Getty Images

RICHIE HAVENS

5:00ᴘᴍ ᴛᴏ 5:45ᴘᴍ

PERFORMANCE FEE:
$6,000

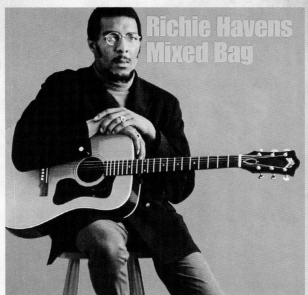

Richie Havens
Mixed Bag

> ## "WE'RE ALL STILL AT WOODSTOCK AS FAR AS I'M CONCERNED."
>
> – RICHIE HAVENS

The Brooklyn-born son of a Native American father and British West Indies mother, Richie Havens (1941–2013) was the oldest of nine children. While his opening-act performance at Woodstock made his career, he was also an actor and a political activist, as well as an entrepreneur who started his own record label. His 1990 autobiography was aptly titled *They Can't Hide Us Anymore*. Havens performed at the first inauguration of President Clinton. With 29 albums to his credit, Havens' only Top 20 hit was "Here Comes The Sun," a 1971 cover of a George Harrison song.

(opposite) Havens' opening set is considered among the finest at Woodstock. Captured in the concert documentary, Havens' moving performance proved a turning point in his career.

SET LIST
1. "From The Prison"
2. "Get Together"
3. "From The Prison (reprise)"
4. "The Minstrel From Gault"
5. "I'm A Stranger Here"
6. "High Flying Bird"
7. "I Can't Make It Anymore"
8. "With A Little Help From My Friends"
9. "Handsome Johnny"
10. "Strawberry Fields Forever"
11. "Hey Jude"
12. "Freedom (Sometimes I Feel Like A Motherless Child)"

PERSONNEL
Richie Havens: vocals / guitar
Daniel Ben Zebulon: percussion
Paul "Deano" Williams: guitar and backing vocals

TOP 5 ALBUMS
Mixed Bag (1966)
Something Else Again (1968)
Alarm Clock (1971)
The End Of The Beginning (1976)
Common Ground (1983)

PPhoto by Michael Ochs Archives/Getty Images

SweetWateR

6:15PM **TO 7:00**PM

PERFORMANCE FEE:
$1,250

Image courtesy Heritage Auctions

> ## "THERE HAS NEVER BEEN ANOTHER WOODSTOCK OR ANOTHER TIME LIKE THAT. IT'S THE REAL DEAL. LITTLE ELSE IS THESE DAYS."
> — nancy "nansi" nevins

T he perennial opening act for The Doors, Eric Burdon & The Animals and a host of their fellow California bands, Sweetwater's rosy future as a true psychedelic folk-rock phenomenon came to an abrupt and premature end when lead singer Nancy "Nansi" Nevins was almost killed in a car crash—only months after Woodstock. Severely injured, Nevins never fully recovered from the accident. A 1999 TV movie, "Sweetwater: A True Rock Story," starred Michelle Phillips as an older Nevins. Sweetwater reunited briefly to play at Woodstock '94 with three original members: Nevins, Fred Herrera and Alex Del Zoppo.

(opposite) In December 1969, only days after appearing on *The Red Skelton Show*, **Nansi Nevens was critically injured in a car accident, putting a screeching halt to the band's future.**

SET LIST

1. "Motherless Child"
2. "Look Out"
3. "For Pete's Sake"
4. "What's Wrong"
5. "Crystal Spider"
6. Two Worlds"
7. "Why Oh Why"
8. "Let The Sunshine In"
9. "Oh Happy Day"

PERSONNEL

Nancy "Nansi" Nevins: vocals/guitar
August Burns: cello
Albert Moore: flute
Alan Malarowitz: drums
Elpidio Cobian: congas
Alex Del Zoppo: keyboards
Fred Herrera: bass

COMPLETE DISCOGRAPHY

Sweetwater (1968)
Just for You (1970)
Melon (1971)
Cycles: The Reprise Collection (1999)
Live At Last (2002)

BERT SOMMER

7:15PM TO 8:00PM

PERFORMANCE FEE:
UNKNOWN

Image courtesy Heritage Auctions

> "I WAS INVOLVED IN THE TWO MOST FAMOUS COUNTERCULTURE EVENTS OF THE '60s, *HAIR* AND WOODSTOCK. THAT AND A TOKEN WILL GET YOU ON THE NEW YORK SUBWAY."
>
> — BERT SOMMER

Bert Sommer (1949–1990) came out of pop band The Left Banke, and played the role of Woof in the original cast of the musical *Hair*. (It was his hair featured on the Playbill.) Although his stirring version of Paul Simon's "America" earned the festival's first standing ovation, he was left off the movie and both original *Woodstock* albums. "It would have been instant stardom for him [being in the movie]," said promoter Artie Kornfeld. "He was devastated," said longtime friend Victor Kahn. "Here was the most famous event in the world and he's not getting any credit for it."

While other performers benefited from being captured in the film or on the Woodstock albums, Sommer faded from the national music scene. "Bert didn't get the breaks," Mr. Kahn said. "He knew he was good, but he was sure there was some kind of curse. He was a sensitive guy. I guess it ate at him, but he didn't talk about how he got screwed. He had an enjoyable life." Sommer settled in Albany, New York, where he played in local bands. In 1990, 12 days after a performance in Troy, New York, Sommer died after a long respiratory illness. He was 41. "He was a gentle soul," Kornfeld said.

(opposite) Although Bert Sommer's powerful rendition of Simon & Garfunkel's "America" was a festival favorite, he slipped quietly from the public eye after not appearing in the Woodstock movie or on the soundtrack.

SET LIST
1. "Jennifer"
2. "The Road To Travel"
3. "I Wondered Where You Be"
4. "She's Gone"
5. "Things Are Going My Way"
6. "And When It's Over"
7. "Jeanette"
8. "America"
9. "A Note That Read"
10. "Smile"

PERSONNEL
Bert Sommer: vocals/guitar
Ira Stone: guitar/keyboards
Charlie Bilello: bass

COMPLETE DISCOGRAPHY
The Road To Travel (1968)
Inside Bert Sommer (1970)
Bert Sommer (1970)
Bert Sommer (1977)
The Road To Travel (2004)

FRIDAY, AUGUST 15, 1969

TIM HARDIN

8:45 PM TO 9:30 PM

PERFORMANCE FEE: $2,000

Woodstock 50th Anniversary

TIM HARDIN   EXCLUSIVELY ON VERVE/FOLKWAYS RECORDS

Image courtesy Heritage Auctions

" PEOPLE UNDERSTAND ME THROUGH MY SONGS. IT'S MY ONE WAY TO COMMUNICATE. "

– TIM HARDIN

PERSONNEL

Tim Hardin: vocals/guitar/piano
Richard Bock: cello
Steve "Muruga" Booker: drums
Gilles Malkine: guitar
Glen Moore: bass
Ralph Towner: guitar/piano
Bill Chelf: piano

TOP 5 ALBUMS

Tim Hardin III: Live In Concert (1968)
The Best Of Tim Hardin (1969)
Bird On A Wire (1971)
Nine (1973)
Hang On To A Dream: The Verve Recordings (1994)

One of the more tragic of the Sixties singer/songwriters, Tim Hardin (1941–1980) wrote "Reason To Believe" and "If I Were A Carpenter," two songs that would have kept him wealthy for the rest of his life had it not been for a heroin dependency that ultimately killed him in 1980. He was 39. His music was as fragile and delicate as he was yet contained the kind of universal truth that touches the core of the human spirit.

(opposite) Tim Hardin was in no shape for Woodstock. His timing was off and his voice faltered badly on stage. Hardin's performance was the first big disappointment of the festival.

Photo by Ralph Ackerman/Getty Images

RAVI SHANKAR

10:00 PM TO 10:45 PM

PERFORMANCE FEE: $4,500

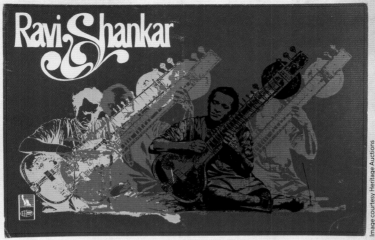

Image courtesy Heritage Auctions

> ## IT MAKES ME FEEL RATHER HURT WHEN I SEE THE ASSOCIATION OF DRUGS WITH OUR MUSIC. THE MUSIC TO US IS RELIGION. THE QUICKEST WAY TO REACH GODLINESS IS THROUGH MUSIC.
>
> – RAVI SHANKAR

The man who taught George Harrison how to play the sitar, Ravi Shankar (1920–2012) had performed successfully at the 1967 Monterey Pop Festival but was reportedly horrified when Jimi Hendrix set his own guitar on fire. "That was too much for me," he told the Associated Press. "In our culture, we have such respect for musical instruments." Still, he was lured to play Woodstock, but cut his set short when it started to drizzle. Honored with dozens of awards, including a Grammy, Shankar was revered in India and influenced musicians worldwide. His daughters, Norah Jones and Anoushka Shankar, have had successful musical careers with Jones earning nine Grammy awards. Shankar died from heart failure in 2012. He was 92.

(opposite) Because of the overt drug use, Ravi Shankar didn't enjoy his Woodstock experience. "I don't like the association of one bad thing with the music," Shankar said.

SET LIST

1. "Raga Puriya-Dhanashri"/ "Gat In Sawarital"
2. "Tabla Solo In Jhaptal"
3. "Raga Manj Kmahaj"

PERSONNEL

Ravi Shankar: sitar
Maya Kulkarni: tambura
Ustad Alla Rakha: tabla

TOP 5 ALBUMS

Portrait of Genius (1964)
Concerto For Sitar & Orchestra (1971)
India's Most Distinguished Musician In Concert (1962)
In Celebration (1996 Box)
The Living Room Sessions (2012)

Photo by Michael Putland/Getty Images

melanie

11:00ᴾᴹ ᴛᴏ 11:30ᴾᴹ

PERFORMANCE FEE:
$750

> ❝ **THE PHENOMENON OF ME AT WOODSTOCK WAS THAT I WALKED ON STAGE AN UNKNOWN PERSON AND I WALKED OFF A CELEBRITY.** ❞
>
> **– MELANIE**

BILL GRAHAM PRESENTS
IN PERSON! IN CONCERT!

TUESDAY
NOVEMBER 16, 1971
8:00 P.M.

BERKELEY COMMUNITY THEATER

TICKETS AT: $3, $4, $5

Ticket outlets:
San Francisco
Tower Records
Columbus & Bay Sts.

Downtown Center Box Office
325 Mason St.

Oakland
Sherman/Clay Box Office
2135 Broadway

Berkeley
Discount Records
Bancroft & Telegraph Ave.

San Jose
San Jose Box Office
912 Town & Country Village

Menlo Park
Peninsula Box Office
325 Sharon Park Drive

melanie

Photo by Getty Images

Melanie Anne Safka–Schekeryk—known simply as Melanie—came out of the Greenwich Village coffee house scene fully formed. She needed no band. Her clarion call of a voice needed no microphone. Her infectious laugh, combined with a good-natured and instantly likeable personality, made her a folkie darling. Woodstock made her a star and the song she wrote and recorded with The Edwin Hawkins Singers about her Woodstock experience, "Lay Down" (Candles In The Rain)" became an instant worldwide classic. She enjoyed a string of 1970s hits such as "Brand New Key," a cover of the Rolling Stones' "Ruby Tuesday" and "The Nickel Song." Of late, she's teamed up with Miley Cyrus in a charitable project, "Happy Hippie," to benefit homeless lesbian, gay, bisexual and transgender youth.

(opposite) Singer–songwriter Melanie was only 22 when she took the Woodstock stage, offering up a performance that would make her famous.

Photo by Bettmann/Getty Images

FRIDAY, AUGUST 15, 1969 ★

RLO GUTHRIE

12:00ᵃᵐ TO 12:45ᵃᵐ

PERFORMANCE FEE:
$5,000

Photo by David Fenton/Getty Images

Arlo Guthrie, performing at the National Mobilization to End the War, Washington, D.C., November 15, 1969.

" THE NEW YORK STATE THRUWAY'S CLOSED, MAN! FAR OUT! "

– ARLO GUTHRIE

With those words, Arlo Guthrie kicked off his set, instantly endearing himself to Woodstock Nation. One of folk music legend Woody Guthrie's eight children, Arlo has been a hippie icon ever since, with an annual Thanksgiving show that's like an American Alternative Institution where he stretches out his rambling counterculture "Alice's Restaurant" to surrealistic and hilarious lengths. Guthrie's biggest hit was a cover of Steve Goodman's "City Of New Orleans." More impressive to many is the work of his Guthrie Center, a nonprofit interfaith church with outreach programs for victims of AIDS and Huntington's Disease. His mother, Marjorie Guthrie, danced for the Martha Graham Company, and founded The Committee To Combat Huntington's Disease, a disease that killed Woody at the age of 55 in 1967).

(opposite) Arlo Guthrie's presence at Woodstock was significant. He was prominently featured in the documentary film, thus propelling his career well beyond "Alice's Restaurant."

Photo by Fotos International/Getty Images

FRIDAY, AUGUST 15, 1969 ★

JOAN BAEZ

1:30am **TO 2:15**am

PERFORMANCE FEE:
$10,000

> # "I'm not interested in talking about music. If there's a choice between people picking and singing in one room and a group of mothers of disappeared Argentinians in another room, I'm gonna go and talk to the mothers."
>
> – Joan Baez

JOAN BAEZ

SPECIAL ADDED CONCERT (SUN. SOLD OUT)

TUESDAY · APRIL 18 · 8:30 PM
BERKELEY COMMUNITY THEATRE · ALL SEATS RESERVED

TICKETS $4.75, 3.75, 2.75
SAN FRANCISCO AND MAIL ORDERS: BERKELEY: ASUC Box Office, Campus Records, Record City
Downtown Center Box Office, 325 Mason, S.F. (Mail orders — Enclose self-addressed, stamped Envelope)
OAKLAND: Sherman-Clay
Presented by Manuel A. Greenhill · Produced by Barry Olivier

Image courtesy Heritage Auctions

Could there be a more saintly or respected figure in all of folk music than the legendary Joan Baez? From her humble beginnings as a New England folkie to her 2017 induction into the Rock and Roll Hall of Fame, Joan Chandos Baez, is a force-of-nature. Born in 1941, Baez was instrumental in the early success of Bob Dylan. The two were kindred spirts and for a brief time they were lovers. She's taken songs from the likes of the Allman Brothers, Stones, Beatles, Paul Simon, Stevie Wonder, The Band, Ryan Adams, Phil Ochs and Steve Earle and made them her own. Her 1975 "Diamonds And Rust" was covered by heavy metal band Judas Priest, proving her music knows no genre limitation.

(opposite) Joan Baez's Woodstock performance was immortalized in the documentary and on the soundtrack album, but she didn't need the career boost: Baez was already beloved.

SET LIST
1. "Oh Happy Day"
2. "The Last Thing On My Mind"
3. "I Shall Be Released"
4. "No Expectations"
5. "Joe Hill"
6. "Sweet Sir Galahad"
7. "Hickory Wind"
8. "Drug Store Truck-Driving Man"
9. "I Live One Day At A Time"
10. "Take Me Back To The Sweet Sunny South"
11. "Let Me Wrap You In My Warm And Tender Love"
12. "Swing Low Sweet Chariot"
13. "We Shall Overcome"

PERSONNEL
Joan Baez: vocals/guitar
Richard Festinger: guitar
Jeffrey Shurtleff: guitar/vocals

TOP 5 ALBUMS
Joan Baez Volume #2 (1961)
Joan Baez (1960)
Any Day Now (1968)
Diamonds and Rust (1975)
Blessed Are... (1971)

QUILL

12:15ᴾᴹ TO 12:50ᴾᴹ

PERFORMANCE FEE:
$375

> ❝ MY DAD WAS IN A BAND, QUILL, WHO OPENED THE SECOND DAY OF WOODSTOCK, THEN FELL INTO OBSCURITY. AND HE NEVER TALKED ABOUT IT. ❞
>
> – AMANDA COLE, DAUGHTER OF JON COLE

Founded by singer/songwriter brothers Jon and Dan Cole, Quill played extensively in the Northeast and was known as a popular opening act for The Who, The Kinks, Janis Joplin, The Velvet Underground and other prominent bands touring the area. After opening for Johnny Winter at the legendary New York City venue Steve Paul's Scene (which included a late-night jam with Jimi Hendrix and Stephen Stills), they were asked to open the second day of Woodstock – after having performed all week for the workers setting up the stage, mental patients in hospitals and prisoners in jail. Known for handing out percussion instruments to the first few rows of their audiences, Quill's creativity and propensity to jam made them a cult favorite. Ahmet Ertegun snatched them up for his Atlantic subsidiary Cotillion Records. Unfortunately, when Quill's Woodstock set was left out of the *Woodstock* documentary and subsequent soundtracks, their debut album received no promotion and quickly fell into the bargain bins of record stores. Cotillion refused to release their second album and the band's meteoric ride was over almost before it started. After taking center stage at the world's most famous concert, the band became but a footnote to rock history.

(opposite) While Woodstock was just the beginning for many artists, it proved to be the beginning of the end for Quill, a Boston-based band rarely remembered today.

SET LIST
1. "They Live The Life"
2. "That's How I Eat"
3. "Driftin'"
4. "Waitin' For You"

PERSONNEL
Jon Cole: bass/vocals
Dan Cole: vocals/trombone/percussion
Roger North: drums/percussion
Norman Rogers: guitar/vocals/percussion
Phil Thayer: keyboards/flute/saxophone/percussion

ONLY ALBUM
Quill (1970)

Photo by Michael Ochs Archives/Getty Images

Photo by Michael Ochs Archives/Getty Images

COUNTRY JOE McDONALD

1:00 PM TO 1:30 PM

PERFORMANCE FEE:
$0

> ## "THE PERFORMANCE ITSELF WAS AN ACCIDENT. I WAS SITTING ONSTAGE, AND THEY BASICALLY FORCED ME TO GO OUT THERE WITH MY GUITAR AND PLAY."
>
> – COUNTRY JOE McDONALD

E. J. D. Enterprises, Inc. Proudly Presents . . .

"WOODSTOCK"
COUNTRY JOE
I - FEEL - LIKE - I'M - FIXIN - TO - DIE - RAG

SHOW & DANCE
Saturday Nite **FEB. 20** Saturday Nite

SALEM ARMORY AUD.
SALEM, OREGON

Showtime **8:30**   Advance Tickets Meier & Frank Salem--$3.00   Doors Open **8:00**

E.J.D. Brings YOU The BEST SHOWS In Oregon for Over 7 Years

Image courtesy Heritage Auctions

As a sailor stationed in Japan, the Washington DC-born Joseph Allen "Country Joe" McDonald wrote songs. As a street performer in Berkeley, California, he added humor and anti-war sentiment to his repertoire. As the leader of Country Joe & The Fish, he became one of the more beloved rock stars of the 1960s and the political conscience of Woodstock Nation. In 1967, McDonald sang at "Human Be-In," ushering in the so-called Summer of Love. Those were heady times, strolling San Francisco's Haight-Ashbury with then girlfriend Janis Joplin. Alas, much like a pair of blue jeans, the Summer of Love faded, as did their romance. Even so, at the request of Joplin, McDonald wrote a song for her.

Finding McDonald hanging out nearby on the second day of Woodstock, festival producer John Morris asked him if he would do an acoustic set while Santana's equipment was set up. McDonald grudgingly agreed. With a borrowed guitar, a rope for a guitar strap, dark sunglasses, a green army shirt and bandana holding back his long hair, McDonald took Woodstock by storm. He opened his set with "Janis," the song he wrote for Joplin two years earlier. Few remembered it simply because of the force of McDonald's infamous last song lead-up – the radical call-and-response "Fish Cheer," immortalized in the *Woodstock* movie and soundtrack.

(opposite) Country Joe McDonald wasn't scheduled to perform Woodstock as a solo act. But while the stage was being set up for Santana, McDonald fired up the crowd with a memorable call-and-response bit featuring the F-bomb, assuring his place in Woodstock history.

Photo by Tucker Ransom/Hulton Archive/Getty

SATURDAY, AUGUST 16, 1969 ★

Santana

2:00 PM TO 2:45 PM

PERFORMANCE FEE: $750

> **" YOU CAN TAKE THINGS THAT JIMI HENDRIX TOOK, FROM CURTIS MAYFIELD OR FROM BUDDY GUY FOR EXAMPLE, BECAUSE WE ARE ALL CHILDREN OF EVERYTHING, EVEN PICASSO. BUT IF YOU WANT TO STAND OUT, YOU HAVE TO LEARN TO CRYSTALLIZE YOUR EXISTENCE AND CREATE YOUR OWN FINGERPRINTS. "**
>
> - CARLOS SANTANA

Poster image courtesy Heritage Auctions

SET LIST

1. "Waiting"
2. "Evil Ways"
3. "You Just Don't Care"
4. "Savor"
5. "Jingo"
6. "Persuasion"
7. "Soul Sacrifice"
8. "Fried Neck Bones & Some Home Fries"

PERSONNEL

Carlos Santana: guitar/ vocals/ maracas/cowbell

Gregg Rolie: vocals/ keyboards/ maracas/tambourine/ jingle bells

Jose "Chepito" Areas: percussion/trumpet

Mike Carabello: congas

Michael Shrieve: drums

David Brown: bass

TOP 10 ALBUMS

Abraxas (1969)
Santana (1970)
Caravanserai (1972)
Santana III (1971)
Santana IV (2016)
Supernatural (1999)
Barboletta (1974)
Shaman (2002)
Amigos (1976)
Power Of Peace (2017)

Did any band use its galvanizing set to propel them more to stardom than Santana did at Woodstock? Many say their blistering 45 minutes was the best set of the weekend. Carlos Santana spewed out spirals of electricity that mesmerized, then energized. No less than 53 musicians have come in and out of this band with the sole star being its namesake. Carlos made—and continues to make—world music before the term existed, fusing elements of salsa, hard rock, funk and R&B, and does so with irresistible flair. With over 100 million albums sold (and counting) since 1967, this San Francisco bandleader/guitarist/composer has to be in the conversation as the greatest American rock star. Santana was inducted in the Rock and Roll Hall of Fame in 1998.

(opposite) Mexican-born guitarist Carlos Santana (right) and his Latin-infused, percussion-driven group, wowed the Woodstock crowd. Santana, on the festival stage with bassist David Brown, came to Woodstock a relative unknown and left a star.

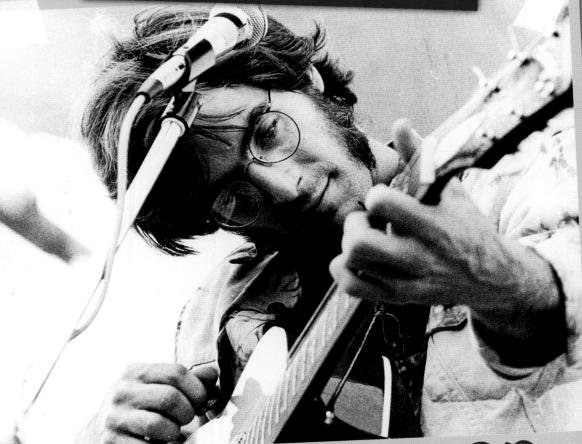

SATURDAY, AUGUST 16, 1969

JOHN SEBASTIAN

Photo by Hulton Archive/Getty Images

3:30 PM TO 4:00 PM

PERFORMANCE FEE:
$1,000

> ## I WENT TO WOODSTOCK as a member OF THE audience. I SHOWED UP WITH a change OF CLOTHES and a TOOTHBRUSH.

— JOHN SEBASTIAN,
REGARDING HIS IMPROMPTU
WOODSTOCK PERFORMANCE

Image courtesy Iconic Auctions

John Sebastian's band The Lovin' Spoonful had broken up prior to Woodstock. He showed up at the festival like everyone else, looking for a good time. "It just so happened that because most of my friends were musicians I ended up backstage," Sebastian said. "There was a moment when the stage had filled up with water and it was impossible to put electric instruments onstage. At that time Chip Monck said to me 'Look, we need somebody who can go out there with an acoustic guitar and hold 'em while we go out and sweep the water off the stage and let it dry up and you're elected.' So, I had to run and borrow a guitar from Timmy Hardin and go on. But, it was not anything I had planned for. It was just one of those nice accidents and it resulted in my career then taking another step forward. Now, I was the Summer Concert Guy. I played every summer concert there was."

Sebastian's free-flowing set let his natural charm shine and his five songs were well received. The native New Yorker, who plays guitar, piano, harmonica and autoharp, and who once turned down an opportunity to join Bob Dylan's band, is influenced by folk and blues yet his legend is firmly rooted in a quasi-jug band style irresistibly rocked up in a soulful mélange of earthy everyman appeal. Sebastian had a surprise No. 1 hit in 1976 with "Welcome Back," the theme song for the TV sitcom *Welcome Back, Kotter.* The Lovin' Spoonful was inducted into the Rock and Roll Hall of Fame in 2000.

(opposite) Near the end of his impromptu performance, John Sebastian encouraged everyone to "clean up a little garbage on your way out and everything is gonna be all right."

SET LIST
1. "How Have You Been"
2. "Rainbows All Over Your Blues"
3. "I Had A Dream"
4. "Darlin' Be Home Soon"
5. "Younger Generation"

PERSONNEL
John Sebastian: vocals/guitar

TOP 5 ALBUMS
Do You Believe In Magic (1965)
with Lovin' Spoonful
Day Dream (1966)
with Lovin' Spoonful
John B. Sebastian (1970)
Welcome Back (1976)
Satisfied (2007)
with David Grisman

SATURDAY, AUGUST 16, 1969

KEEF HARTLEY BAND

4:45 PM TO 5:30 PM

PERFORMANCE FEE: $500

Photo by Michael Putland/Getty Images

> **"DECCA RECORDS GOT US ON TO THE WOODSTOCK FESTIVAL. IT ALL HAPPENED SO FAST. IT WAS A NEW LINE-UP AND WE WERE VERY UNDER-REHEARSED. WE DID NOT PLAY AS WELL AS WE COULD AND DIDN'T EVEN USE OUR OWN INSTRUMENTS, WHICH WE HAD TO BORROW FROM SANTANA. IT WAS A MISSED OPPORTUNITY FOR THE BAND."**
>
> – GUITARIST
> MILLER ANDERSON

British drummer Keef Hartley (1944–2011) replaced Ringo Starr in Rory Storm & The Hurricanes when Ringo became a Beatle. The longtime John Mayall Bluesbreaker also led his own bands, one of which, The Keef Hartley Band, had him oftentimes dress up as an American Indian in full head dress and war paint. His sound was pre-fusion jazz-rock and his band appeared positioned for success. Although relatively unknown, the band proved a solid choice for Woodstock. Unfortunately, when the band's manager demanded $2,000 up front to sign a release, Michael Wadleigh's *Woodstock* film crew wasn't able to film the Keef Hartley Band's set. The band also missed out on the *Woodstock Soundtrack* album, ultimately dooming it to fall between the cracks of notable out-sized rock personalities.

(opposite) The Keef Hartley Band was relatively unknown when it played Woodstock. Despite a spirited and well-received performance, the band failed to gain much fame or recognition as a result of their festival appearance.

SET LIST
1. "Spanish Fly"
2. "She's Gone"
3. "Too Much Thinkin'"
4. "Believe In You"
5. "Rock Me Baby"
6. "Sinnin' For You/Leaving Trunk/Just To Cry/Sinnin' For You (reprise)

PERSONNEL
Keef Hartley: drums
Miller Anderson: guitar/vocals
Jimmy Jewell: saxophone
Henry Lowther: trumpet/violin
Gary Thain: bass

TOP 5 ALBUMS
Half Breed (1969)
Lancashire Hustle (1973)
Dog Soldier (1975)
Crusade (1967) with John Mayall
Ten Years Are Gone (1973) with John Mayall

Photo by Tucker Ranson/Pictorial Parade/Hulton Archive/Getty Images

THE INCREDIBLE STRING BAND

6:00pm TO 6:40pm

PERFORMANCE FEE: $4,500

"I REMEMBER WHEN WE PLAYED AT WOODSTOCK THAT THEY DIDN'T EVEN HAVE COVER FOR THE STAGE, NO DRESSING ROOMS, NOTHING, AND THE ONLY FOOD AVAILABLE WAS CHAMPAGNE AND STRAWBERRIES."

— MIKE HERON,
GUITARIST,
THE INCREDIBLE
STRING BAND

The Incredible String Band had a cup of coffee as one of the hippest acts in the world. Their ephemeral music was delicate and seemingly profound with a gentle sound that would waft through the air and disappear like smoke from a cigarette. Starting their psychedelic folk music journey in 1966 Scotland, they added sophisticated layers of sound that actually influenced the course of international underground pop and even the burgeoning world music movement. First breaking up in 1974, they reformed in 1996 before breaking up for good in 2006.

Originally scheduled to play Friday evening with fellow folk acts, the band refused to play in the rain and were rescheduled for Saturday. It was a bad move. The crowd, ready for hard rock, never warmed to the traditional folk sound. The Incredible String Band was not included in the *Woodstock* movie or soundtrack album, meaning many were unaware that they had even been at the festival.

(opposite) The Incredible String Band performing at the Woodstock festival (from left to right): Rose Simpson, Mike Heron, Christina "Licorice" McKechnie and Robin Williamson.

SET LIST
1. "Invocation"
2. "The Letter"
3. "Gather 'Round"
4. "This Moment"
5. "Come With Me"
6. "When You Find Out Who You Are"

PERSONNEL

Mike Heron: guitar/piano/vocals/percussion
Robin Williamson: guitar/piano/violin/vocals
Christina "Licorice" McKechnie: percussion/vocals
Rose Simpson: bass/recorder/vocals/percussion

TOP 5 ALBUMS

The Incredible String Band (1966)
The 5000 Spirits or the Layers of the Onion (1967)
The Hangman's Beautiful Daughter (1968)
Changing Horses (1969)
Be Glad For The Song Has No Ending (1971)

Photo by Michael Ochs Archives/Getty Images

CANNED HEAT

7:30PM **TO 8:30**PM

PERFORMANCE FEE:
$6,500

Image courtesy Heritage Auctions

> # "I MUST BE THE ONLY GUY WHO DIDN'T GET LAID AT WOODSTOCK."
>
> — DRUMMER ADOLFO "FITO" DE LA PARRA

Arguably one of Woodstock's most fun-filled hours, California's Canned Heat rocked so hard with the boogie beat that Woodstock Nation rose as one and stayed on their feet throughout, dancing and romancing to some of the wildest shuffles and jump-blues you're likely to hear. Called a rural-hippie anthem, "Going Up the Country" became the band's best-known song. Sure, Canned Heat may not own any of their own songs, but they continue to tour today with their original rhythm section, one of the greatest drum/bass combos ever, intact.

Photo by Tucker Ranson/Pictorial Parade/Hulton Archive/Getty Images

(opposite) When introduced at Woodstock, Bob "The Bear" Hite informed the audience that Canned Heat was "just gonna play a little blues!" And, with bassist Larry Taylor (above) showing the band meant business, Canned Heat proceeded to blow the crowd away.

SET LIST

1. "I'm Her Man"
2. "Going Up The Country"
3. "A Change Is Gonna Come/ Leaving This Town"
4. "Too Many Drivers At The Wheel"
5. "I Know My Baby"
6. "Woodstock Boogie"
7. "On The Road Again"

PERSONNEL

Alan "Blind Owl" Wilson: guitar/ harmonica/vocals
Bob "The Bear" Hite: vocals/ harmonica
Harvey "The Snake" Mandel: guitar
Larry "The Mole" Taylor: bass
Adolfo "Fito" de la Parra: drums

TOP 5 ALBUMS

Canned Heat (1967)
Boogie With Canned Heat (1968)
Future Blues (1970)
One More River To Cross (1973)
Hallelujah (1969)

Photo by GAB Archive/Redferns/Getty Images

mountain

9:00ᴘᴹ ᴛᴏ 10:00ᴘᴹ

PERFORMANCE FEE: **$2,000**

> **"IT WAS INCRED-IBLE, MAN. I WAS SO SCARED. I GOT UP ONSTAGE AND I HAD MY THREE STACKS OF SUNN AMPS. FELIX HAD HIS THREE STACKS OF SUNNS AS WELL. IT WAS SO LOUD! WHEN IT CAME TIME FOR MY SOLO, OUR ROADIE HOOKED UP ALL TWELVE OF THE SUNNS."**
>
> – LESLIE WEST,
>   LEAD GUITAR,
>   MOUNTAIN

PERSONNEL

Leslie West: guitar/vocals
Felix Pappalardi: bass/ vocals
Norman D. Smart II: drums
Steve Knight: keyboards

TOP 5 ALBUMS

Mountain was a band that lasted less than three years but left an impenetrable mark on rock history. Bassist Felix Pappalardi had produced Cream. His technical studio wizardry coupled with his onstage look and feel was the perfect counterpoint to Leslie West's thunderous lead guitar. The extreme volume of a Mountain concert caused Pappalardi to retire early due to partial deafness. He would go on write, record, produce and arrange for other artists before being shot dead at the age of 43 by his wife in 1983. West had his right leg amputated in June of 2011 but was right back out on stage within months. His 2015 *Sound Check* album made it to #2 on the *Billboard* blues chart. No, they didn't do "Mississippi Queen" at Woodstock and legendary drummer Corky Laing was a roadie at the time but Mountain's set is generally regarded as one of the best sets of the weekend. Oddly, the band's performance wasn't included in the *Woodstock* documentary or soundtrack album. No matter, Mountain rose to stardom by the sheer force of their music.

(opposite) Woodstock rocked hard Saturday night to the full-frontal assault of Mountain, the Long Island proto-heavy metal band of (from left) Corky Lang, Steve Knight, Felix Pappalardi and Leslie West.

Photo by Malcolm Lubliner/Michael Ochs Archives/Getty Images

SATURDAY, AUGUST 16, 1969

GRATEFUL DEAD

10:45ᴘᴍ ᴛᴏ 12:30ᴀᴍ

PERFORMANCE FEE: $7,500

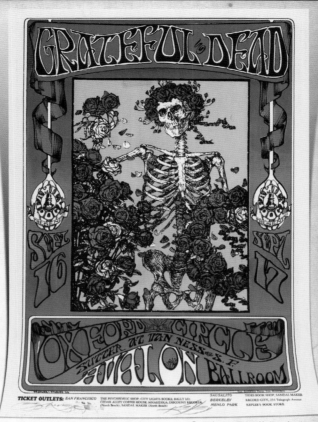

Poster image courtesy Heritage Auctions

> **PEOPLE ARE ALWAYS WANTING ME TO TAKE A STAND ON DRUGS, AND I CAN'T. TO ME, IT'S SO RELATIVISTIC, AND IT'S ALSO VERY PERSONAL. A PERSON'S RELATIONSHIP TO DRUGS IS LIKE THEIR RELATION-SHIP TO SEX.**
>
> – JERRY GARCIA

The 13 musicians who have floated in and out of the Grateful Dead since 1965 have all participated in a grand communal experiment. They were known to offer concert-goers LSD (their sound man back in the day was none other than Owsley Stanley, the chemist who produced massive amounts of the drug). In 1987, their admission of a "Touch Of Grey" went Top 10. Deadheads, as their rabid fans are known, are famous for following the band around the globe. As for the Dead's Woodstock performance, it was mostly forgettable. The weather, technical problems and long meandering jams all left the crowd disappointed, disinterested or asleep.

(opposite) The Grateful Dead, (from left) Jerry Garcia, Phil Lesh, Bob Weir, Bill Kreutzmann and Mickey Hart, are known for hit-or-miss perfromances. Some concerts are transcendent. As for their Woodstock set? Definitely a long, strange trip.

SET LIST
1. "St. Stephen"
2. "Mama Tried"
3. "Dark Star"
4. "High Time"
5. "Turn On Your Love Light"

PERSONNEL
Jerry Garcia: guitar/vocals
Bob Weir: guitar/vocals
Bill Kreutzmann: drums/percussion
Mickey Hart: drums/percussion
Ron "Pigpen" McKernan: keyboards/harmonica/congas/vocals
Tom Constanten: keyboards/vocals
Phil Lesh: bass

TOP 5 ALBUMS
American Beauty (1970)
Workingman's Dead (1970)
In The Dark (1987)
Terrapin Station (1977)
Blues For Allah (1975)

Photo by Michael Ochs Archives/Getty Images

Photo by Michael Ochs Archives/Getty Images

SATURDAY, AUGUST 16, 1969

CREEDENCE CLEARWATER REVIVAL

1:00ᵃᵐ TO 1:50ᵃᵐ

PERFORMANCE FEE:
$10,000

> **"WE WEREN'T THAT GOOD, ALTHOUGH MY SON SAYS SOME OF THOSE GUITAR SOLOS WERE INCREDIBLE, BUT PEOPLE WEREN'T REACTING TO US. THE GRATEFUL DEAD PUT EVERYBODY TO SLEEP."**
>
> – JOHN FOGERTY

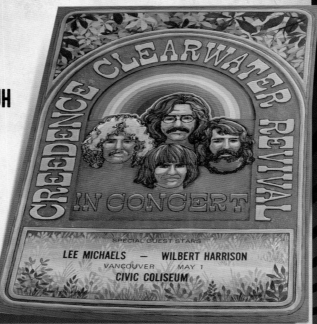

Poster image courtesy Heritage Auctions

John Fogerty was in rare form as he led his California crew in what history has proven to be one of the better sets of Woodstock. Back in the day, a live act was judged by how close they sounded to the record. In that sense, Creedence Clearwater Revival was absolutely perfect. To the dismay of the rest of the band, Fogerty refused to allow any of CCR's set in the *Woodstock* movie or soundtrack. While the decision did little to derail their spectacular rise to stardom, fans often forget Creedence was at Woodstock.

The band started as a high school cover band in 1959 as Blue Velvet, changed their name to The Golliwogs as more and more original songs entered the set, finally becoming CCR in 1968 when radio jumped all over their cover of a 1956 Dale Hawkins rockabilly song, "Suzie Q." They followed it up with another 1956 hit cover, "I Put A Spell On You" by Screaming Jay Hawkins. A steady stream of hit albums followed until Tom Fogerty quit the band in 1970 over younger brother John's refusal to allow his band mates any creative control whatsoever. By 1972 the band was done. Yet the music remains timeless and vital. Bassist Stu Cook and drummer Doug "Cosmo" Clifford still tour and play the band's great songs. John Fogerty, the band's lead singer, lead guitarist and principle songwriter, went on to a successful solo career. CCR was inducted into the Rock and Roll Hall of Fame in 1993.

(opposite) In the late '60s and early '70s, Creedence Clearwater Revival weren't the hippest American band, just the best. Few recall CCR playing Woodstock because John Fogerty refused to allow their performance to be included in the movie or soundtrack.

SET LIST
1. "Born On The Bayou"
2. "Green River"
3. "Ninety-Nine and a Half (Won't Do)"
4. "Commotion"
5. "Bootleg"
6. "Bad Moon Rising"
7. "Proud Mary"
8. "I Put A Spell On You"
9. "Night Time Is The Right Time"
10. "Keep On Chooglin'"
11. "Suzie Q"

PERSONNEL
John Fogerty: vocals/guitar/harmonica
Tom Fogerty: rhythm guitar
Doug "Cosmo" Clifford: drums
Stu Cook: bass/keyboard

TOP 5 ALBUMS
Green River (1969)
Bayou Country (1969)
Creedence Clearwater Revival (1968)
Willie and the Poor Boys (1969)
Cosmo's Factory (1970)

JANIS JOPLIN

2:30ᵃᵐ TO 3:30ᵃᵐ

PERFORMANCE FEE: $7,500

Photo by Bettmann/Getty Images

Poster image courtesy Heritage Auctions

> ❝ **HOW ARE YOU OUT THERE? YOU OK? YOU'RE STAYING STONED? YOU GOT ENOUGH WATER? YOU'VE GOT A PLACE TO SLEEP? WE GOT TO REMEMBER, THE MUSIC IS GROOVING, MAN! IT'S NOT MEANT TO PUT YOURSELF THROUGH BAD CHANGES. YOU DON'T HAVE TO TAKE ANYBODY'S SHIT JUST TO LIKE THE MUSIC. YOU KNOW WHAT I MEAN? ❞**
>
> – JANIS JOPLIN,
> FROM THE WOODSTOCK STAGE

Janis Lyn Joplin (1943-1970), a ballsy, swaggering Texas misfit who hid her massive insecurities underneath her ultra-tough veneer, found a small sense of happiness upon being convinced to move to San Francisco where she joined a ragtag group of longhairs called Big Brother & The Holding Company. They burst on the scene so powerfully that Janis was immediately thrust into playing a boozehound rock star role and she lived up to it in spades, ultimately leaving the band for solo glory that didn't last long. A little more than a year after playing Woodstock, Joplin died October 4, 1970, of an accidental heroin overdose. Her second album, *Pearl*, was released posthumously the following year and featured the classic hit, "Me And Bobby McGee," a cover of a Kris Kristofferson tune.

(opposite) Joplin's Woodstock set with the Kozmic Blues Band — not Big Brother & The Holding Company — wasn't received well. For unknown reasons, her performance wasn't included in the original *Woodstock* movie or soundtrack.

SET LIST

1. "Raise Your Hand"
2. "As Good As You've Been To This World"
3. "To Love Somebody"
4. "Summertime"
5. "Try (Just A Little Bit Harder)"
6. "Kozmic Blues"
7. "Can't Turn You Loose"
8. "Work Me, Lord"
9. "Piece Of My Heart"
10. "Ball And Chain"

PERSONNEL

Janis Joplin: vocals
Maury Baker: drums
Terry Clements: tenor saxophone
Cornelius "Snooky" Flowers: baritone saxophone/vocals
Luis Gasca: trumpet
John Till: guitar
Richard Kermode: keyboards
Brad Campbell: bass

TOP 5 ALBUMS

Cheap Thrills (1968)
I Got Dem Old Kozmic Blues Again, Mama! (1969)
Big Brother & The Holding Company (1967)
Pearl (1971)
Greatest Hits (1973)

Photo by Michael Ochs Archives/Getty Images

SLY & THE FAMILY STONE

4:00ᵃᵐ TO 5:00ᵃᵐ

PERFORMANCE FEE:
$7,000

> ## GET UP OFF YOUR FEET AND SAY 'HIGHER' AND THROW THE PEACE SIGN UP! IT'LL DO YOU NO HARM!
>
> — SLY STONE

Image courtesy Heritage Auctions

One of the most groundbreaking of all the Sixties acts, San Francisco's Sly & The Family Stone featured male and female, black and white musicians playing a brand of funk-rock that had yet to be fully explored by anyone to that point. Thanks to the hit single "Everyday People," by the time they made Woodstock the band was one of the hottest in America. Their set is generally regarded as one of the best of the weekend, opening with a horn burst that woke up those already asleep. Soon the crowd was dancing crazily and shouting back at the stage when asked if they wanted to be taken higher. The inclusion of "I Want to Take You Higher" in the *Woodstock* documentary and soundtrack solidified the band's fame. From its 1966 inception to its 1983 demise, this family stayed together throughout Sly's drug addiction and descent into mental illness. Sly & The Family Stone were inducted into the Rock and Roll Hall of Fame in 1993.

(opposite) Sly Stone's unstable life and erratic career might well serve as a music business cautionary tale, but his energetic Woodstock performance spoke to the brilliance of the man and his band at the height of their powers.

SET LIST
1. "M'Lady"
2. "Sing A Simple Song"
3. "You Can Make It If You Try"
4. "Everyday People"
5. "Dance To The Music"
6. "Music Lover"
7. "I Want To Take You Higher"
8. "Love City"
9. "Stand!"

PERSONNEL
Sly Stone: vocals/keyboard/harmonica
Rose Stone: vocals/keyboards
Freddie Stone: vocals/guitar
Cynthia Robinson: trumpet
Greg Errico: drums
Larry Graham: bass
Jerry Martini: saxophone

TOP 5 ALBUMS
Dance To The Music (1968)
Stand! (1969)
There's A Riot Goin' On (1971)
Life (1968)
A Whole New Thing (1967)

Photo by Archive Photos/Getty Images

THE WHO

5:30ᵃᵐ TO 6:35ᵃᵐ

PERFORMANCE FEE: $6,250

"F*CK OFF! F*CK OFF MY F*CKING STAGE."

- PETE TOWNSHEND TO ACTIVIST ABBIE HOFFMAN BEFORE BOOTING HIM OFF THE WOODSTOCK STAGE DURING THE WHO'S SET.

Image courtesy Heritage Auctions

BILL GRAHAM PRESENTS IN NEW YORK

PERFORMING THEIR ENTIRE ROCK-OPERA

TOMMY

Presented By Special Arrangement With Her Majesty Queen Elizabeth II

JOSHUA LIGHT SHOW

MONDAY THROUGH SATURDAY OCTOBER 20-25, 1969

FILLMORE EAST

Those who were still up at this ungodly hour got to see the classic rock-opera *Tommy* in its entirety. Just as memorable was the sight of Pete Townshend kicking political activist Abbie Hoffman off the stage. During a break following "Pinball Wizard," Hoffman walked onto the stage, grabbed a microphone and announced that the festival was meaningless as long as White Panther Party leader and MC-5 manager John Sinclair was rotting in prison. Townshend cut him off, encouraging Hoffman to get the "f*ck off" the stage. Then, for good measure, he cracked Hoffman in the back of the head with his guitar.

The Woodstock experience changed The Who forever. "Playing large-scale things like Woodstock turned us into superstars," Townshend said. "In some ways it was wonderful... But in other ways it was disarming because the natural easy connection between me, as the writer, and the audience, was broken. The feeling I had was that we were starting to become in a way like Tommy: we started to become more deeply deaf, dumb and blind to what was actually happening to us."

The Who were inducted into the Rock and Rock Hall of Fame in 1990 and has long been considered one of the greatest rock bands of all time.

(opposite) Arriving at the festival on the heels of their massive hit single "Pinball Wizard," The Who's early-morning, raucus performance was a highlight of the Woodstock documentary and soundtrack album, solidifing their reputation as extraordinary live performers.

SET LIST
1. "Heaven And Hell"
2. "I Can't Explain"
3. "It's A Boy"
4. "1921"
5. "Amazing Journey"
6. "Sparks"
7. "Eyesight To The Blind"
8. "Christmas"
9. "Acid Queen"
10. "Pinball Wizard"
11. "Do You Think It's Alright"
12. "Fiddle About"
13. "There's A Doctor"
14. "Go To The Mirror"
15. "Smash The Mirror"
16. "I'm Free"
17. "Tommy's Holiday Camp"
18. "We're Not Gonna Take It"
19. "See Me Feel Me"
20. "Summertime Blues"
21. "Shakin' All Over"
22. "My Generation"
23. "Naked Eye"

PERSONNEL
Roger Daltrey: vocals
Pete Townshend: guitar/vocals
John Entwistle: bass/vocals
Keith Moon: drums

TOP 5 ALBUMS
Tommy (1969)
Quadrophenia (1973)
Who's Next (1971)
The Who Sell Out (1967)
My Generation (1965)

Photo by Getty Images

JEFFERSON AIRPLANE

7:00ᵃᵐ TO 8:45ᵃᵐ

PERFORMANCE FEE:
$7,500

> **"EVERYBODY HAD BEEN UP FOR 24 HOURS, HAD 18,000 DIFFERENT DRUGS, WERE IN SUN AND RAIN, AND WEREN'T FUNCTIONING AT TOP LEVEL. THERE'S NO BIG REASON TO BE IN A MOVIE JUST BECAUSE YOU'RE THERE. THERE SHOULD BE SOME KIND OF PERFORMANCE AND IT WAS PRETTY BAD. BETWEEN THE SOUND AND THE VISUALS, PEOPLE KEPT GOING TO SLEEP."**

– GRACE SLICK

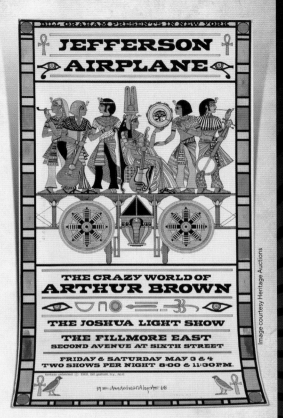

Image courtesy Heritage Auctions

Fronted by the wonderfully trippy and beguiling Grace Slick, Jefferson Airplane epitomized the San Francisco psychedelic scene of the 1960s. Their music and attitude defined an era. They were intended to headline Saturday evening but instead took the stage early Sunday morning in what Slick referred to as the "morning maniac music" slot. After being awake for nearly 24 hours and ingesting plenty of drugs, their performance was uneven and at times ragged. The most rabble-rousing political band of San Francisco scene, Jefferson Airplane could never again equal its legendary eight-year run from 1965 to 1972. But they did achieve far more commercial success, morphing into Jefferson Starship in 1974, an evolution that led to fifteen Top 40 hits. Original singer Signe Anderson and original singer/songwriter/guitarist Paul Kantner died on the same day, January 28, 2016. Jefferson Airplane was inducted into the Rock and Roll Hall of Fame in 1996.

(opposite) At the ungodly hour of 7:00 Sunday morning, Jefferson Airplane took the stage to close Saturday's endlessly long day of performances. The band's set was both frazzled and spirited, after having partied enthusiastically while waiting their turn.

SET LIST
1. "The Other Side Of Life"
2. "Somebody To Love"
3. "3/5 of a Mile in 10 Seconds"
4. "Won't You Try/Saturday Afternoon"
5. "Eskimo Blue Day"
6. "Plastic Fantastic Lover"
7. "Wooden Ships"
8. "Uncle Sam Blues"
9. "Volunteers"
10. "The Ballad Of You And Me And Pooneil"
11. "Come Back Baby"
12. "White Rabbit"
13. The House at Pooneil Corners"

PERSONNEL
Grace Slick: vocals/tambourine/maracas
Marty Balin: vocals/tambourine/maracas
Paul Kantner: guitar/vocals
Jorma Kaukonen: guitar/vocals
Jack Casady: bass
Spencer Dryden: drums
Nicky Hopkins: piano

TOP 5 ALBUMS
Volunteers (1969)
Surrealistic Pillow (1967)
Crown Of Creation (1968)
After Bathing At Baxter's (1967)
Jefferson Airplane Takes Off (1966)

JOE COCKER
& THE GREASE BAND

2:00ᴾᴹ TO 3:30ᴾᴹ

PERFORMANCE FEE:
$1,375

AP Photo

> **WE WERE KIND OF LUCKY BECAUSE WE GOT ON STAGE REAL EARLY. IT TOOK ABOUT HALF THE SET JUST TO GET THROUGH TO EVERYBODY, TO THAT KIND OF CONSCIOUSNESS. YOU'RE IN A SEA OF HUMANITY AND PEOPLE AREN'T NECESSARILY LOOKING TO ENTERTAIN YOU. WE DID 'LET'S GO GET STONED' BY RAY CHARLES, WHICH KIND OF TURNED EVERYBODY AROUND A BIT, AND WE CAME OFF LOOKING PRETTY GOOD THAT DAY.**
>
> – JOE COCKER

Image courtesy Heritage Auctions

For many, Joe Cocker's set was the most memorable of the festival. Happening on a brilliantly sunny Sunday afternoon and kicking off the final day of Woodstock, Cocker's performance was stunning. The sky darkened almost directly afterwards, the winds whipped up, the announcement came of no more music for awhile, and then, of course, the deluge. After Cocker, it was survival mode for all concertgoers.

John Robert "Joe" Cocker (1944-2014) always loved Ray Charles. The Englishman grew up imitating Charles and matured into the kind of vocalist whose spastic stage mannerisms and air guitar were often imitated but never duplicated (except for maybe John Belushi). A brilliant interpreter of other artists, Cocker took from The Beatles, Billy Preston, Leon Russell, Bob Dylan, The Box Tops, Otis Redding, Sam & Dave, The Rolling Stones, Traffic and even turned the 1955 Julie London hit "Cry Me A River" into a vehicle for his onstage drama and the serious phlegm of his over-the-top vocals. His 1970 "Mad Dogs And Englishmen" tour is among the most celebrated of all the rock touring circuses.

(opposite) Joe Cocker's backing band, The Grease Band, played two songs and then Cocker stepped center stage, opening his hour-and-a-half set with the Bob Dylan song "Dear Landlord," dedicated to Max Yasgur.

SET LIST

1. "Dear Landlord"
2. "Something Comin' On"
3. "Do I Still Figure In Your Life"
4. "Feelin' Alright"
5. "Just Like A Woman"
6. "Let's Go Get Stoned"
7. "I Don't Need No Doctor"
8. "I Shall Be Released"
9. "Hitchcock Railway"
10. "Something To Say"
11. "With A Little Help From My Friends"

PERSONNEL

Joe Cocker: vocals
Henry McCullough: guitar/ backing vocals
Alan Spenner: bass/backing vocals
Chris Stainton: keyboards/ backing vocals
Bruce Rowland: drums

TOP 5 ALBUMS

Mad Dogs & Englishmen (1970)
With A Little Help From My Friends (1969)
I Can Stand A Little Rain (1974)
Joe Cocker! (1969)
Cocker (1986)

SUNDAY, AUGUST 17, 1969

★ SUNDAY, AUGUST 17, 1969 ★

COUNTRY JOE & THE FISH

6:30PM TO 7:50PM

PERFORMANCE FEE: $2,500

Photo by Hulton Archive/Getty Images

Image courtesy Heritage Auctions

> **"GIMME AN F! GIMME A U! GIMME A C! GIMME A K! WHAT'S THAT SPELL? WHAT'S THAT SPELL? WHAT'S THAT SPELL?"**

– COUNTRY JOE McDONALD, FROM THE WOODSTOCK STAGE

After performing solo on Saturday, and following a three-hour rain delay, Country Joe McDonald was joined with his band for a rollicking Sunday evening performance. Country Joe & The Fish, San Francisco's most overtly political band, returned to sooth the soaked denizens of Woodstock Nation after an interminable wait. Born out of the 1965 Berkeley on-campus free-speech movement, the band was a true hippie montage of psychedelia, angry folk-rock rave-ups, long distorted guitar and organ solos and propensity for jug-band melancholy. When the '60s ended, however, so did the band. As a solo artist, Country Joe soldiered on to far greater success thanks in large part to his Woodstock performance.

(opposite) Country Joe & The Fish featured Joe McDonald (seated, second from left) and Barry "The Fish" Melton (standing). McDonald and Melton connected over a shared love of folk music, particularly the protest music of Woody Guthrie.

PERSONNEL

Country Joe McDonald: guitar/harmonica/kazoo/ vocals
Barry "The Fish" Melton: guitar/vocals
Greg "Duke" Dewey: drums
Mark Kapner: keyboards/organ
Doug Metzler: bass

TOP 5 ALBUMS

Electric Music For The Mind And Body (1967)
I Feel Like I'm Fixin' To Die (1967)
Together (1968)
Here We Are Again (1969)
CJ Fish (1970)

Photo by Michael Putland/Getty Images

TEN YEARS AFTER

8:30PM TO 9:30PM

PERFORMANCE FEE:
$3,250

> **" THE SUNDAY STORM IS STILL ONE OF THE HIGHLIGHTS OF THE FESTIVAL TO ME. GOD'S OWN LIGHT SHOW. THE STAGE GOT FLOODED AND THERE WERE SPARKS JUMPING AROUND. IN FACT, NOBODY WANTED TO GO ON. THEY THOUGHT IT WAS DANGEROUS. I TOOK A WALK AROUND THE LAKE AND KIND OF JOINED IN THE AUDIENCE AS IT WERE, WHICH WAS GREAT. I GOT TO SEE IT FROM THE OTHER SIDE OF THE FENCE. "**
>
> **– ALVIN LEE, TEN YEARS AFTER**

Photo by Tom Copi/Michael Ochs Archives/Getty Images

Led by the lightning-fast lead guitarist/lead singer Alvin Lee (1944-2013), Ten Years After stormed through the blues upon their 1960 inception as Ivan Jay & The Jaycats. Many years and many names later, their self-titled 1967 debut set the scene for a seven-year run of non-stop touring and recording wherein they placed no less than 11 albums on charts from both sides of the Atlantic. Woodstock, while hardly overwhelming for Lee, proved a great boost for the band. "It was a good festival, a big deal personally," Lee said. "Actual playing-wise it didn't seem that special. It was just basically another gig. We were doing 5,000-seaters a year after Woodstock, and when the movie came out we were kind of catapulted to the 20,000-seat bracket." Lee left the band in 1974, in open rebellion against the pop direction that his label and band mates wanted, thus ending the band's most popular run.

(opposite) No doubt Woodstock raised the profile of the English blues-rock band Ten Years After dramatically. The band was helped further by the inclusion of "I'm Going Home" in Michael Wadleigh's festival documentary film and its accompanying soundtrack album.

SET LIST
1. "Spoonful"
2. "Good Morning Little Schoolgirl"
3. "Hobbit"
4. "I Can't Keep From Crying Sometimes"
5. "Help Me"
6. "Going Home"

PERSONNEL
Alvin Lee: guitar/vocals
Leo Lyons: bass
Chick Churchill: organ
Ric Lee: drums

TOP 5 ALBUMS
Undead (1968)
Ssssh (1969)
Ten Years After (1967)
Stonedhenge (1969)
Cricklewood Green (1970)

Photo by Gijsbert Hanekroot/Redferns

THE BAND

10:00PM TO 10:50PM

PERFORMANCE FEE:
$7,500

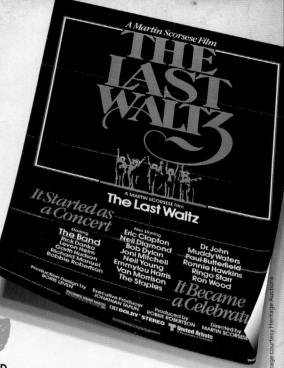

Image courtesy Heritage Auctions

> ❝ **I WISH WE'D BEEN ABLE TO PUT OUT 20 ALBUMS AND PLAY TWICE AS MUCH AND TOUCH TEN TIMES AS MANY PEOPLE, BUT I DON'T HAVE ANY REGRETS.** ❞
>
> **– LEVON HELM (1940-2012), DRUMMER/VOCALIST, THE BAND**

From 1958 to 1963, rockabilly legend Ronnie Hawkins hired the members of what would become The Band individually as his backup, The Hawks. Five years later, they would dub themselves The Band, but not before also being Bob Dylan's backup. Once their self-titled debut hit the charts, all bets were off as the four Canadians and lone American, drummer Levon Helm, from Turkey Scratch, Arkansas, became the darlings of what would, years later, be called Americana Roots-Rock. Even George Harrison wanted to quit The Beatles and join The Band.

Their run would continue only until 1976 when acrimony and drugs took over, resulting in the departure of main songwriter/lead guitarist Robbie Robertson. The Band left a living legacy due in large part to the filming of their "farewell concert appearance" by Martin Scorsese on Thanksgiving day in 1976 at the Winterland Ballroom in San Francisco. Scorsese's documentary, entitled *The Last Waltz*, is a rock classic featuring guest appearances from Bob Dylan, Eric Clapton, Ringo Starr, Ronnie Wood, Muddy Waters, Van Morrison, Neil Young, Ronnie Hawkins, Joni Mitchell and a host of other stars. The Band was inducted into the Rock and Roll Hall of Fame in 1994.

(opposite) From left: Garth Hudson, Robbie Robertson, Levon Helm, Richard Manuel and Rick Danko of The Band.

SET LIST

1. "Chest Fever"
2. "Don't Do It"
3. "Tears Of Rage"
4. "We Can Talk"
5. "Long Black Veil"
6. "Don't You Tell Henry"
7. "Ain't No More Cane"
8. "This Wheel's On Fire"
9. "I Shall Be Released"
10. "The Weight"
11. "Loving You Is Sweeter Than Ever"

PERSONNEL

Robbie Robertson: guitar/vocals
Rick Danko: bass/vocals
Levon Helm: drums/vocals/mandolin
Garth Hudson: organ/piano/clavinet/synthesizer/saxophone
Richard Manuel: piano/organ/vocals/drums

TOP 5 ALBUMS

The Band (1969)
Music From Big Pink (1968)
Northern Light Southern Cross (1975)
Cahoots (1971)
Stage Fright (1970)

Photo by Michael Ochs Archives/Getty Images

SUNDAY, AUGUST 17, 1969

JOHNNY WINTER

12:00ᵃᵐ TO 1:10ᵃᵐ

PERFORMANCE FEE:
$3,750

Still Alive and Well

Johnny Winter

Special Guests:
Stories

Mid South Coliseum
FRIDAY, Dec. 14
8:00 P.M.

Ticket Locations
Budget Tapes & Records.
Music Location (Southbrook Mall)
Raleigh Springs Mall Information Center.

Popi's.

Mid South Coliseum Box Office.
Goldsmith's Central Ticket Office.
Village Records (Parkway Village)

Image courtesy Heritage Auctions

> ## "OUR MANAGER AT THE TIME, STEVE PAUL, DIDN'T WANT US IN THE MOVIE OR ON THE SOUNDTRACK. I FORGET WHY."

– JOHNNY WINTER (1944-2014)

In 1969, Columbia Records gave the albino blues man Johnny Winter $600,000, the largest advance ever to that point...and he delivered. Catapulting Texas Blues into the national consciousness, he went on to have a 45-year career filled with famous jams (some with Joplin and Hendrix), incendiary live performances and dozens of great records. At Woodstock, Johnny was joined by his brother, Edgar, on sax and piano for the last several songs of the set, including "I Can't Stand It" and a ten-minute version of "Tobacco Road." The latter song became a staple of Edgar's own concerts in the Seventies. While not included in the *Woodstock* documentary or on the soundtrack, eight songs Johnny Winter performed at the concert were featured on *The Woodstock Experience* album released in 2009. Johnny died in 2014, still on the road, finally clean after a decades-long heroin addiction.

(opposite) Johnny Winter's manager didn't want him filmed for the Woodstock movie. He feared a negative association. "He told us people would forget all about Woodstock," says Edgar Winter. "The only thing people forgot is that Johnny and I performed at Woodstock!"

SET LIST

1. "Mama, Talk To Your Daughter"
2. "Leland Mississippi Blues"
3. "Mean Town Blues"
4. "You Done Lost Your Good Thing Now/Mean Mistreater"
5. "I Can't Stand It"
6. "Tobacco Road"
7. "Tell The Truth"
8. "Johnny B. Goode"

PERSONNEL

Johnny Winter: vocals/guitar
Edgar Winter: keyboards/alto saxophone/vocals
Tommy Shannon: bass
"Uncle" John Turner: drums

TOP 5 ALBUMS

Johnny Winter (1969)
Second Winter (1969)
The Progressive Blues Experiment (1968)
Guitar Slinger (1984)
Roots (2011)

Photo by Tad Hershorn/Hulton Archive/Getty Images

BLOOD, SWEAT & TEARS

1:45ᵃᵐ TO 2:45ᵃᵐ

PERFORMANCE FEE: $15,000

Image courtesy Heritage Auctions

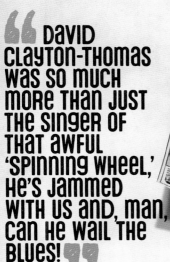

DaVID CLAYTON-THOMAS WAS SO MUCH MORE THAN JUST THE SINGER OF THAT AWFUL 'SPINNING WHEEL,' HE'S JAMMED WITH US AND, MAN, CAN HE WAIL THE BLUES!

– FITO DE LA PARRA, DRUMMER, CANNED HEAT

Over 150 musicians—including such jazz legends as Randy Brecker, Joe Henderson, Bernard "Pretty" Purdie and Jaco Pastorius—have floated in and out of Blood, Sweat & Tears for the last 50 years. It was drummer Bobby Columby who got the bright idea to fuse rock 'n' roll, intricately ornate pop arrangements with brass on their Al Kooper-led 1967 debut, *Child Is Father To The Man*. Kooper left and Canadian David Clayton-Thomas was brought in as lead vocalist. The new Blood, Sweat & Tears released a self-titled album in January 1969. The album was smoother and more traditionally melodic, featuring such hits as "You've Made Me So Very Happy," "Spinning Wheel" and "When I Die." The LP sold ten million copies and earned a Grammy as Album of the Year. Like others excluded, people forget the band played Woodstock because Blood, Sweat & Tears were not in the festival documentary or on the soundtrack.

(opposite) Blood, Sweat & Tears, from left, guitarist Steve Katz, bass guitarist Jim Fielder, singer David Clayton-Thomas, trombonist Jerry Hyman and trumpeters Chuck Winfield and Lew Soloff.

PERSONNEL

David Clayton-Thomas: vocals
Bobby Colomby: drums
Jim Fielder: bass
Dick Halligan: keyboards/trombone/flute
Jerry Hyman: trombone/recorder
Steve Katz: guitar/harmonica/vocals
Fred Lipsius: alto sax/piano
Lew Soloff: trumpet/flugelhorn
Chuck Winfield: trumpet/flugelhorn

TOP 5 ALBUMS

Child Is Father To The Man (1967)
Blood, Sweat & Tears (1968)
Greatest Hits (1972)
In Concert (1976)
B, S & T 4 (1971)

Photo by Fotos International/Getty Images

CROSBY, STILLS, NASH & YOUNG

3:30am TO 5:00am

PERFORMANCE FEE:
$5,000

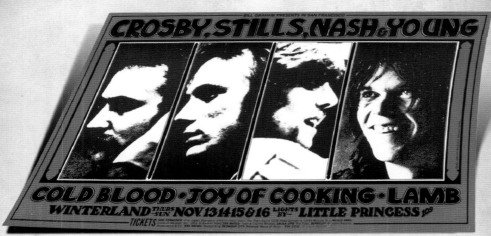

Image courtesy Heritage Auctions

"IT'S OUR SECOND GIG AND WE'RE SCARED SHITLESS."

– STEPHEN STILLS

When Graham Nash left The Hollies, Great Britain and his wife to discover the joys of Southern California, harmonizing with David Crosby and Stephen Stills at a party and falling in love with Joni Mitchell, rock history was set in stone. Enter Neil Young, fresh off feuding with Stills in Buffalo Springfield, but always up for an adventure, and truly the die was cast. Woodstock was Crosby, Stills, Nash & Young's second gig. It was memorable, in part because Young is forgotten. Young refused to be shot for the *Woodstock* film and most historical documents of the event concentrated on CSN, not CSNY. "There were three days of really good music and the movie was three hours," Nash said. "So there are a lot of great performances that have never been seen apart from bootlegs." The first CSNY album, *Déjà Vu*, was a smash hit in 1970 and featured the Joni Mitchell-written song, "Woodstock." Together, CSNY was a musical banquet filled with glorious harmonies and thundering electric guitars. They were also combustible as hell, splitting acrimoniously after a summer tour. Young is not a band guy, and has been in and out of the group ever since. Nash and Crosby aren't talking these days. Stills, one of the more underrated lead guitarists in all of rock, proved himself in a variety of genres but never reached the heights set years before. When the four convened in the late Sixties, magic happened.

(opposite) Graham Nash and David Crosby of Crosby, Stills, Nash & Young perform on stage at Woodstock, which marked just the the group's second show together.

ACOUSTIC SET LIST

1. "Suite: Judy Blue Eyes"
2. "Blackbird"
3. "Helplessly Hoping"
4. "Guinnevere"
5. "Marrakesh Express"
6. "4 + 20"
7. "Mr. Soul"
8. "Wonderin'"
9. "You Don't Have To Cry"
10. "Find The Cost Of Freedom"
11. "49 Bye-Byes"

ELECTRIC SET LIST

12. "Pre-Road Downs"
13. "Long Time Gone"
14. "Bluebird"
15. "Sea Of Madness"
16. "Wooden Ships"

PERSONNEL

Stephen Stills: guitar/vocals/organ/piano/percussion
David Crosby: guitar/vocals
Graham Nash: guitar/vocals/organ/percussion
Neil Young: guitar/vocals/organ/piano
Greg Reeves: bass
Dallas Taylor: drums

TOP 5 ALBUMS

Déjà Vu (1970)
Crosby, Stills & Nash (1969)
CSN (1977)
Daylight Again (1982)
CSN 2012 (2012)

Photo by Michael Ochs Archives/Getty Images

SUNDAY, AUGUST 17, 1969

PAUL BUTTERFIELD BLUES BAND

6:00am TO 7:15am

PERFORMANCE FEE: NOT AVAILABLE

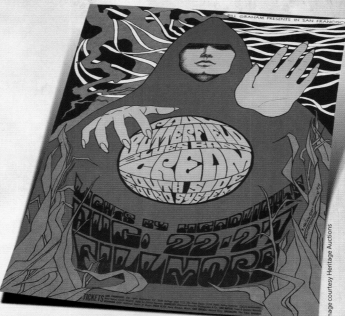

Image courtesy Heritage Auctions

SET LIST

1. "Born Under A Bad Sign"
2. "No Amount Of Loving"
3. "Driftin'"
4. "Morning Sunrise"
5. "All In A Day"
6. "Love March"
7. "Everything's Gonna Be Alright"

PERSONNEL

Paul Butterfield: harmonica/vocals

Howard "Buzzy" Feiten: guitar

Rod Hicks: bass

Ted Harris: keyboards

Phillip Wilson: drums

Steve Madaio: trumpet/percussion

Keith Johnson: trumpet/percussion

David Sanborn: alto saxophone/percussion

Trevor Lawrence: baritone saxophone/percussion

Gene Dinwiddie: tenor saxophone/percussion/vocals

TOP 5 ALBUMS

East-West (1966)

The Paul Butterfield Blues Band (1965)

The Resurrection Of Pigboy Crabshaw (1967)

In My Own Dream (1968)

Keep On Moving (1969)

> **HE HAD THE WHOLE BLUES SENSIBILITY, MUSICALITY AND APPROACH DOWN PAT. HE JUST WENT FOR IT AND TOOK IT ALL IN, AND HE EMBODIED THE ESSENCE OF WHAT THE BLUES WAS ALL ABOUT. UNFORTUNATELY, HE LIVED THAT WAY A LITTLE TOO MUCH.**
>
> – MARIA MULDAUR ON PAUL BUTTERFIELD

The original Paul Butterfield Blues Band in 1963 was a dynamic Chicago Blues collective led by Butter, as Paul Butterfield (1942-1987) was known on the mean streets when he used to play for chump change and start fights. When the late guitar genius Michael Bloomfield joined in '64, the band had unlimited potential. Unfortunately, by '69, Butter had a new crew, thus wasting his window of impending superstardom. Still, he continued with new versions of the band on into solo outings, all spectacularly received and heralded as the real deal when it came to the blues. Bloomfield died in 1981 of a drug overdose at the age of 37, as did Butterfield six years later at 44. Paul Butterfield Blues Band was inducted into the Rock and Roll Hall of Fame in 2015.

(opposite) Sandwiched between Crosby, Stills, Nash & Young and the novelty act, Sha Na Na, the Paul Butterfield Blues Band was not included in the Woodstock film or album.

SUNDAY, AUGUST 17, 1969

SHa na na

7:45ᵃᵐ TO 8:15ᵃᵐ

PERFORMANCE FEE:
$700

Photo by Gems/Redferns/Getty Images

Photo by Richard E. Aaron/Redferns/Getty Images

❝OVER HALF A MILLION PEOPLE INHALED OVER 60 TONS OF MARIJUANA BUT THERE WAS NO CRIME AND NOT ONE REPORTED CASE OF GLAUCOMA.❞

– HENRY GROSS,
LEAD GUITARIST,
SHA NA NA

The most incongruous band of all to perform at Woodstock had to have been the doo-wop novelty act known as Sha Na Na. They took their name from the 1958 Silhouettes hit "Get A Job" which goes "Get a job sha na na na sha na na na na." The doo-wop group started as an a capella group at Columbia University. Pure entertainers, they were song 'n' dance men who wore gold lamé, leather, pompadour hairstyles and parodied the songs of the 1950s with choreography, humor and great vocals. They were so new, that when they played Woodstock their debut album had not yet been released. Despite a whole new cast, Sha Na Na continue to tour today.

(opposite) Sha Na Na were entertaining as hell. The group's image and style were unabashedly anachronistic, covering '50s pop and doo-wop standards, with slicked-back hair in greaser fashion and dressed in flamboyant outfits.

SET LIST
1. "Get A Job"
2. "Come Go With Me"
3. "Silhouettes"
4. "Teen Angel"
5. "Jailhouse Rock"
6. "Wipe Out"
7. "Blue Moon"
8. "(Who Wrote) The Book Of Love"
9. "Little Darlin'"
10. "At The Hop"
11. "Duke Of Earl"
12. "Get A Job" (reprise)

PERSONNEL
Joe Witkin: keyboards/vocals
Jocko Marcellino: drums
Donny York: vocals
Rob Leonard: vocals
Alan Cooper: vocals
Dennis Greene: vocals
Dave Garrett: vocals
Richie Joffe: vocals
Scott Powell: vocals
Henry Gross: guitar
Bruce Clarke III: bass
Elliot Cahn: guitar

TOP 5 ALBUMS
Rock'n'Roll Is Here To Stay (1969)
Sha Na Na (1971)
Sha Na Na Now (1975)
Sha Na Na Is Here To Stay (1977)
Rockin In The Eighties (1980)

Photo by Jim Marshall/courtesy Heritage Auctions

SUNDAY, AUGUST 17, 1969

JIMI HENDRIX

9:00ᵃᵐ TO 11:15ᵃᵐ

PERFORMANCE FEE: $18,000

> ## WHEN THE POWER OF LOVE OVERCOMES THE LOVE OF POWER THE WORLD WILL KNOW PEACE.
> — JIMI HENDRIX

Gered Mankowitz/courtesy Heritage Auctions

Jimi Hendrix was born Johnny Allen Hendrix, November 27, 1942, in Seattle, only to be renamed James Marshall by his father, James "Al" Hendrix. Somehow it seems fitting that the man who changed rock 'n' roll would himself undergo an abrupt change at such an early age. Unable to read or write music, Jimi Hendrix nonetheless created a new musical form by combining fuzz, feedback and controlled distortion with showmanship and an undeniable sexuality that electrified audiences. Hendrix (1942–1970) made it so big in London after being in the road bands of The Isley Brothers and Little Richard, that American audiences presumed he was British. Hendrix ignited the rock world with his stunning performance at the 1967 Monterey International Pop Music Festival, a performance that concluded with him setting his Stratocaster on fire. Although Hendrix was scheduled to headline Woodstock's Sunday offerings, he was pushed back to Monday morning when most everybody had gone home. Erroneously introduced as "The Jimi Hendrix Experience" (that band had already broken up), Jimi's jam buddies for this gig must've looked out in the morning sunshine at a sea of garbage with but a few stragglers still roaming around. Estimates range from 35,000 to 45,000 for Jimi out of the half-million. No matter the size of the audience, Hendrix's performance at Woodstock, especially his remarkable distortion-drenched rendition of "The Star-Spangled Banner," has become one of the defining moments in rock history.

(opposite) Jimi Hendrix's blazing performance at Monterey in 1967 was matched at Woodstock, where his chilling and monumental version of "The Star-Spangled Banner" electrified what remained of the festival crowd.

SET LIST
1. "Message To Love"
2. "Hear My Train A'Comin'"
3. "Spanish Castle Magic"
4. "Red House"
5. "Mastermind"
6. "Lover Man"
7. "Foxy Lady"
8. "Jam Back At The House"
9. "Izabella"
10. "Gypsy Woman/"Aware Of Love"
11. "Fire"
12. "Voodoo Child (Slight Return)/"Stepping Stone"
13. "The Star-Spangled Banner"
14. "Purple Haze"
15. "Woodstock Improvisation"
16. "Villanova Junction"
17. "Hey Joe"

PERSONNEL
Jimi Hendrix: guitar/vocals
Billy Cox: bass
Larry Lee: rhythm guitar/vocals
Mitch Mitchell: drums
Juma Sultan: congas
Jerry Velez: congas

TOP 5 ALBUMS
Electric Ladyland (1968)
Are You Experienced? (1967)
Axis: Bold As Love (1967)
Band Of Gypsies (1970)
First Rays of the New Rising Sun (1997)

CHAPTER FIVE

A PATCHWORK QUILT OF HUMANITY

About 30 minutes after Country Joe's solo set, the unknown Santana made music history. As wonderful and fun as Country Joe's set was, Woodstock Nation was in no way prepared for the onslaught of the sublime Santana, a band that manager Bill Graham had to strong-arm onto the festival if it wanted the Grateful Dead. Guitarist Carlos Santana, heavily tripping on mescaline, a popular '60s psychedelic drug akin to LSD, rose to the occasion, foreshadowing a legendary career as one of music's true virtuosos and guiding lights. Santana exploded onto the scene with an epic set at Woodstock. The group's performance was a testimony for the power of togetherness and youth, with 20-year-old drummer Michael Shrieve's amazing solo during "Soul Sacrifice" highlighting a transcendent show.

Michael Shrieve: "I was so young. We were all so young. I will never, ever, forget the feeling of total and complete awe while flying in that helicopter [to

A feeling of total and complete awe swept over Santana drummer Michael Shrieve while taking in the Woodstock audience.

the festival] and seeing all those people. It really felt to me, at that exact moment, like there was something incredible going on and I was going to be part of it. I was so in the moment. It felt like it was something people did not expect to be happening and it was totally, irrevocably overwhelming. I knew, in the air, I would be participating in something really special and that people would be talking about it for decades, maybe centuries. I mean, hey, we're talking about it now, aren't we? How long ago was it? About 100 years ago, right? The fact that I knew I was right in the middle of it was like feeling that I was at the center of the universe. And for that small period of time, I was!"

Carlos Santana: "I don't even think our debut album was out yet. I do remember that gig, though. All of it. We had just played with Buddy Miles and he was so upset that day at The Singer Bowl [the former stadium in Queens, New York] about a week before Woodstock. There were these two transvestite Jimi Hendrix lookalikes and I was like, 'whoa! This is a different kind of city.' It was New York and I was used to San Francisco. Woodstock was only our fourth gig as a band. Another thing I remember about being in New York for those two gigs was hearing 'Jingo' on the radio for the first time. Any artist will

Bassist David Brown (left) performs with the other members of Santana, including drummer Michael Shrieve, bandleader Carlos Santana (with guitar, center), and percussionists Michael Carabello and Jose Areas at Woodstock.

tell you that the first time they hear their tunes on the radio is a big deal. That's so true."

Michael Shrieve: "I'll tell you, in our defense, I think the thing that served us well as a band that day was that we played to each other. It wasn't as if we were all thinking, 'oh shit, there's half a million people out there.' That wasn't it at all. We just played to each other in a tight little circle. That worked for us. It always worked for us. The difficult thing about it was that we didn't even have a record out yet. No one there was familiar with our music or even aware of us as a band."

Carlos Santana: "People would be going oh-my-god, it's an out-of-body experience, what Shamans call a 'rebirthing,' a giving birth to a new perception, a new sensation, a new vision. What is a human being without a vision? A toaster! A microwave oven!"

Michael Shrieve: "With no record out, we really had to win over those people on our raw presentation. I think we succeeded because it was such a tribal feeling, both on stage and in the audience. Everybody felt connected that day. Everybody felt special just being there with each other. You could feel it. There was a definite palpable sense of togetherness in the air. Hey, we introduced ourselves to the world that day!"

Carlos Santana: "I've come to understand the necessity of balance. Charlie Parker played Mexican songs ["La Cucaracha"]. John Coltrane did Broadway songs ["My Favorite Things" from *The Sound Of Music*]. Miles Davis covered Cyndi Lauper ["Time After Time"],

Michael Jackson ["Human Nature"] and Walt Disney ["Someday My Prince Will Come" from *Snow White & The Seven Dwarfs*]. People have to have songs! There's a whole lotta people who want you to keep going in the other direction and get lost in the desert improvising because they want to get lost with you. There's already plenty of that. We can certainly go out there enough and people say, 'wow, that's amazing. I've never heard that before.' That's exactly what they said after we performed at Woodstock. The secret, if there is such a thing to the glory of music, is willingness to be open...a willingness to trust.

"All we're asking when you come out is to bring intense enthusiasm and don't let your ego get in the way of the band or you won't be here long. Keep the water clear of any color. Like a diamond. All the colors are already there. Put sunlight on a diamond? Whew! All the colors appear instantly. Take it away from the sun and it's clear. That's what I've always wanted from the musicians in my band. Bring your clarity and abide by the tempo, the feel and the groove. That's what creates memorable music. I want everyone to say the same thing you said when you told me you saw me opening for Buddy Miles at the Singer Bowl and then perform at Woodstock a week later so many years

> "WITH NO RECORD OUT, WE REALLY HAD TO WIN OVER THOSE PEOPLE ON OUR RAW PRESENTATION. I THINK WE SUCCEEDED BECAUSE IT WAS SUCH A TRIBAL FEELING, BOTH ON STAGE AND IN THE AUDIENCE."
> — MICHAEL SHRIEVE

Drummer Michael Shrieve was only 20 when he blew away the crowd with his solo work in "Soul Sacrifice" during Santana's set.

Tucker Ranson/Pictorial Parade/Hulton Archive/Getty Images

Carlos Santana came to Woodstock a relative unknown; he left a star.

Photo by Tucker Ransom/Hulton Archive/Getty

ago. We want to make things memorable.

"Way prior to those two back-to-back gigs in August of 1969, the '60s was when I had really spent considerable time learning all about Mahatma Gandhi, the Black Panthers, Cesar Chavez, the Peace and Freedom Movement on through Dr. Martin Luther King, Jr., Arthur Ashe and Harry Belafonte. These are the people I look up to. Then, when I reached the same plateau with humility, I kept looking at them for further inspiration. Y'know, it was true what I learned as a child. It's not so much how many zeroes are on your paycheck. What matters is how you carry yourself. Integrity. Elegance. They don't sell that on Rodeo Drive. There's no garment you can buy that will bring you those things."

While Santana came to Woodstock a relative unknown, Creedence Clearwater Revival were one of the few bands that had already achieved significant success on the Billboard charts. Creedence's hour-long set was like a greatest hits album, with "Bad Moon Rising" and "Proud Mary" both having reached No.2 on the Billboard Hot 100. As they walked on stage just after midnight on Saturday, their current single, "Green River," was at No.15, its third week on the U.S. chart.

"By the time we got to Woodstock," John Fogerty said later, "I felt we were the number one band. Assuming that The Beatles were God, I thought that we were the next thing under them."

Creedence drummer Doug Clifford: "There was a distinct possibility that if we didn't accept the invitation to Woodstock, there would have been no festival at all! All the big bands were waiting on the sidelines not confirming their participation until at least one major band said yes. These promoters were new. They had no track record. We were that band. Nobody drew as many people as we did in '69. So after some major deliberation, we decided that, hell yeah, we liked the idea of what they were attempting. The second we said yes, and word got out, all the other bands fell into line. It was like a race to swim across the lake. They just needed somebody to start it. So we started it. Had we not, it might not have happened, or, there might not have been such a great roster of talent. Thus, there might not have been so many people and it might not have been such a cultural milestone."

In the summer of 1969, CCR had already played the Newport Festival in California, the Denver and the Atlanta festivals, along with the Atlantic City Festival. So when the band was to be helicoptered into the site, Woodstock was to be simply another big festival. Or so they thought.

The night before Woodstock, CCR appeared on "The Andy Williams Show," along with Ray Charles. The TV show was recorded in advance of airing on NBC in October. Unfortunately, the show was besieged with technical problems, turning the recording into a marathon session. Wrapping up things late, Creedence caught a red-eye flight from California to New York for the festival.

Doug Clifford: "So we get off the red-eye all bleary-eyed and pissed-off at the previous night's TV problems. We had

A couple enjoys the show atop a custom-painted VW Bus named "Light."

AP Photo

some locals who agreed to drive us from the airport to the backstage area... but they couldn't do it. The roads were jammed. People had abandoned their cars all over the highway. The only way in and out for us was a two-man helicopter carrying three. It was one of those little bubble-top things that looks like a dragonfly. The pilot was in the left seat, John [Fogerty] was half sitting on what was in-between the seats, and I was scrunched up in the right seat, not being able to shut the damn door because my leg was still outside the helicopter. I wound up holding the door in place because otherwise it would start flapping around and probably would have been ripped off. I was more than a little nervous.

"So there I am holding on to John's seat belt with my left hand and holding on to the door for dear life with my right hand. I kept trying to move my left leg closer to John and that's the position the three of us were in when we took off. Tom [Fogerty] and Stu [Cook] were waiting back at the airport for their turn.

"As we cleared the perimeter [of the Woodstock grounds], I looked down and that's when I realized just how big this event was. I couldn't believe it. We'd done a lot of festivals before that one. I mean, hell, 1969 was the year of the big festivals. We'd played to over 15,000

American filmmaker Michael Wadleigh (shirtless, right) and his wife and film crew member Renee Wadleigh (left) stand on the stage during Woodstock. Behind them, in the background, is one of the festival organizers, Michael Lang (in dark vest, with hand on hip).

folks at a pop so we had an idea in our minds what we were getting ourselves into and what it would look like. The sun was going down. It couldn't have been a more dramatic scene in a movie. The copter wasn't flying very high at all. As we cleared this rise in the topography, the sun was setting on the crowd, which really accentuated the many colors. So we come up over this rise and I remember shouting OH MY GOD. It was a patchwork quilt of humanity stretching out in every direction that the eye could see. John and I just looked at each other and then down at the crowd again. There was nothing else to say."

John Fogerty (in his autobiography, *Fortunate Son*): "I actually went walking out in the crowd. Had a little hat on, and kind of hid. Somebody was selling water—a gallon for $5. And I was aghast. That was so mercenary to me, that somebody was making money off water. So I came back to the guys even more nervous. I was worried that all these people would get moving in a stampede and that people would get hurt. Even though we were the so-called peace and love generation, we'd never been tested that way. I didn't want something bad to happen because all the naysayers—starting with President Nixon—would just go, 'See? I told ya! Make no mistake about that: you people are just no good!'"

Creedence bassist Stu Cook: "Woodstock was overwhelming. All you could see from the stage was teeth and hair. We didn't even have any spotlights. The weather had created dangerous electrical shock possibilities. We followed the [Grateful] Dead and they meandered on and on as they were wont to do until we took the stage to a ton of technical problems due to the weather and people being stoned, I guess. The usual. I just kept my head down and played, hoping the tech stuff would be worked out and we'd all be the better for it. It was a bit of a task. We were a well-rehearsed band. We were what we were, so it wasn't hard for us to play these songs, even under the conditions. That's why I thought we had a really good set while so many other artists didn't. They got into the party. We saved the party for after the show. That was always how we did it."

Doug Clifford: "Today, it's all looked back on with fondness because of the historical nature of the event itself. Back then, though, yeah, we had our share of equipment problems. I mean, it wasn't major, but we certainly had a few. Still, we had a pretty basic format. We had it down to a fine science. We were just gonna do what we did no matter what. We were fortunate to get everything up and running. Sure, there were little snippets here and there that we were well aware of but we soldiered through. That's what professionals do. The show must go on! I thought we played just fine.

Stu Cook: "Being from the Bay Area, I'd seen the Dead many times. They were never my kind of band. I remember thinking backstage, 'when do WE

Jerry Garcia called The Grateful Dead's Woodstock set "a total disaster ... best left forgotten."

Photo by Archive Photos/Getty Images

get to go to work? Is there going to be anybody awake?' Fortunately, there was a terrific audience. Most people misunderstand Woodstock. It wasn't about the music. The film shows it. It was always about the audience."

John Fogerty (in *Fortunate Son*): "We came charging out like we always did, James Brown-style—Bang! We started with 'Born On The Bayou.' By the second number I was looking around and I saw...nothing. Blackness. Shadow, but no movement. I finally looked closer, because you can really only see the first four rows or so, and it was like a scene from Dante's Inferno, the souls coming out of hell. All these intertwined young people, half nude and muddy, and they looked dead. The Grateful Dead had put a half a million people to sleep."

Doug Clifford: "It was pretty hectic. We were tired. We went on after the Dead and having to wait during their interminably long set was a nightmare. They did 'Turn On Your Love Light' for 45 minutes! Come on, man! They sounded terrible. I mean, geez, we knew them all personally. They're Bay Area guys just like us. They have their thing. It was always more cultish than musical, in my opinion. So sure, they're doing their thing, but there's also a point of approaching rudeness! It was selfish on their part to just keep going and going like that. Hell, we were the headliners!"

Grateful Dead guitarist Jerry Garcia (in Michael Lang's *The Road To Woodstock*): "Jeez, we were awful! We were just plumb atrocious! As a human being, I had a wonderful time hanging out with friends and sharing great little jams. But

When CCR, fronted by John Fogerty, signed on at Woodstock, other acts quickly followed. Such was the influence of the band who, next to The Beatles, Fogery figured was the best in the world.

Koh Hasebe/Shinko Music/Getty Images

"I DIDN'T LOOK AT THE MOVIE AS BEING A HISTORICAL DOCUMENT, THE WAY I MIGHT NOW; I LOOKED AT IT AS A CAREER OPPORTUNITY. I THINK THE PROMOTERS WENT BROKE IMMEDIATELY. SOMEWHERE IN THE VAGUE RECESSES OF MY MIND I'M NOT EXACTLY SURE THAT WE ACTUALLY GOT PAID FOR PLAYING WOODSTOCK."

– JOHN FOGERTY

our performance onstage was musically a total disaster that is best left forgotten."

Grateful Dead's Bob Weir (in *The Road To Woodstock*): "Some people made their careers at Woodstock, but we spent about 20 years making up for it. It was probably the worst set we've ever performed."

John Fogerty: "So I walked up to the mic and said something to the effect of, 'well, we're havin' a great time up here. Hope you're havin' fun out there.' No response. Dead audience. Could've heard a pin drop. And finally some guy a quarter mile away in the distant night flicked his lighter, and I heard him say ever so faintly, 'don't worry about it, John! We're with you!' So I played the rest of the set for that one guy. I was connecting with somebody—that's all I cared about."

It was a memorable night for Creedence, but one that's been mostly forgotten by everyone else since Fogerty, the band's driving force as songwriter, lead singer and lead guitar, wouldn't allow the performance to be included in the Woodstock documentary.

Stu Cook: "We weren't in the film because of John's bad decision. Nobody really appreciated the phenomenon at the time. We should've been in the film. Every band in the film got to get at least one good song out of it, even those who had to have the songs fixed in the studio. I was part of the process. I know how that whole thing came together technically. All that aside, we weren't included, despite having at least a half-dozen studio-quality tracks from that concert. There were many options available to the film producers. Every band in that

film received a major bump to their career. Bill Graham practically had to pay to get Santana on that bill. And their 'Soul Sacrifice' broke the band. Look at Ten Years After! A mid-level British blues band became rock stars."

John Fogerty: "I didn't look at the movie as being a historical document, the way I might now; I looked at it as a career opportunity. I think the promoters went broke immediately. Somewhere in the vague recesses of my mind I'm not exactly sure that we actually got paid for playing Woodstock."

Stu Cook: "[Director] Michael Wadleigh and I had a very interesting conversation in '94 on the 25th Anniversary [of Woodstock]. He was working on a Director's Cut release. He was in Hong Kong promoting it and told me he really wanted Creedence in the film from the beginning. Then, 25 years later, we get another chance at it, but Fogerty was, again, dead set against it. Still! Twenty-five years later! So I ask Michael, 'can't you just put us in there anyway?' And he goes, 'look, I'm not having my film release [messed] up by a John Fogerty lawsuit. I'm really sorry.' So was I."

John Fogerty: "My mindset [about the movie] was, why should I show the whole world we're doing badly? I didn't think that was going to help us. We were doing great everywhere else."

Stu Cook: "I went to work with a guy named Yves [Beauvais] from Atlantic Records whom Elliot Easton of The Cars introduced me to. Doug and I went behind Fogerty's back and told Yves that Creedence wanted to at least be on the soundtrack for that 25th Anniversary album. Atlantic did no due diligence whatsoever to make sure I was telling the truth and placed five tracks on it! John freaked out, but the deal was done. What was he going to do? Make life miserable for us? He had already done that many times over. For many decades."

Doug Clifford: "Under the circumstances, I thought we did a really good job. But not John. So to not be in the movie for the reasons we were told was a big blow to us. It was just John flexing his muscles. It still hurts every time I think about it. That was such a truly historic set for us. To not be in the film with all our peers? Damn! That movie made a lot of careers for a lot of bands. Granted, we were No. 1 in the world as far as record sales. But that was all the more reason that we should've been in the movie!"

Stu Cook: "After the set, we got out of there, got back to the hotel and wondered how the hell the crew got our equipment out of there and on to the next gig the following day. The roads were horrific. But after playing for half a million people, there we were in some small New Jersey town the next night with The Nitty Gritty Dirt Band playing for less than 500 people. We were still trying to process the night before and it was like, 'oh, back to this level again.' By the time we were the No. 1 band in the world, we were just about to break up. So we're No. 1 in, say, Singapore, but we were done. Three and a

Photo by OAG Archive/Redferns/Getty Images

CCR's set was memorable for the band but largely forgotten after John Fogerty failed to give the thumbs-up for its use in the Woodstock documentary.

half years. That's it. Plus, of course, nine and a half years of scuffling before 'Suzie Q,' our first hit. Those were the years that got us there. Then personalities and circumstances took over."

By late 1972, Creedence Clearwater Revival was done. After scoring nine Top Ten singles in three years, ego-driven power struggles, internal arguments over artistic control and constant bickering over business matters put an end to one of the greatest American bands of all time.

CHAPTER SIX

FREEDOM, MAN, FREEDOM

There was a point Saturday when I started to roam. I knew Neil would hold the spot. I was hot. I knew there was a lake. After Friday night ended so emotionally for me, and so far Saturday afternoon was thrilling/idyllic/stoned-out/breathtaking/enervating, I skipped out on the Keef Hartley Band and the Incredible String Band to go swimming. I was baking. And thirsty. I've always said Woodstock would have been so much easier with bottled water (and cell phones).

The lake was inviting. Topless girls were everywhere. I stood at where the water met the land and gazed out fondly at the bucolic tableau right before my eyes. Should I just splash around in my T-shirt and shorts? Having no idea that tomorrow would be the deluge and my clothing would be soaking wet anyway, and still having no clue as to where the car was with all of our supplies (oh, what I would give for one of my mom's skinny peanut butter and jelly sandwiches now!), I decided to go skinny-dipping, folding my T-shirt, shorts and underwear under my sneakers and white socks which I stashed under a rock for safe keeping. I mean, really, who's going to steal someone else's dirty clothes?

The water was warm and inviting. It felt so good. I noticed a girl staring at me and I swam to her. This was one of those moments-in-time that one remembers forever, a true '60s montage of sun, lake, and the first rush of puppy love. Or was it lust? The advent of five decades might have coated the memory with an unrealistic sheen but I swear we held both hands, looked into each other's eyes, and almost kissed before she laughed and swam away. I followed her.

"Come back with me."

"Where?"
"We have the best spot, right in front of the stage. My friend Neil is holding down the fort and someone planted a flag nearby so it's easy to find. C'mon!"

Clothes were definitely optional as bathers took to the nearby lake to commune with nature and each other.

Visions of love crowded my fragile eggshell psyche.

She laughed.

"I have to get back to my boyfriend."

The world caved in …

It was only Mountain's fourth gig. When they took the stage at the prime-time hour of Saturday night, 9:00, fans saw—after Bob "The Bear" Hite of Canned Heat—yet another 300-pound behemoth creak the floor boards. Lead guitarist Leslie West was a monster shredder. His feedback-soaked shrieks permeated the night sky with drama, flair, theatricality and a prescient heavy metal vibe, like lightning across a black vista. Bassist Felix Pappalardi had a resume filled with production duties for the likes of Cream— he produced both *Disraeli Gears* and *Wheels Of Fire*—plus The Youngbloods on their seminal 1967 hit, "Let's Get Together," a song that charted again in June of '69.

Simply put, Mountain was magnificent. In a weekend where many of the bands couldn't play to their potential due to a variety of factors, Mountain was exemplary, the perfect band, at the perfect time, playing the perfect blend of hard-ass rock, blues and jammy improvisation. They might've been the LOUDEST band I had ever experienced. Felix looked every inch the rock star. We had no way of knowing that backstage, Mountain had ingratiated themselves with their fellow rock stars by bringing numerous roasted chickens to share.

Felix's wife Gail had written lyrics for Cream and Mountain, and it's her

Leslie West (right) and Felix Pappalardi of Mountain rocked Woodstock Nation hard and LOUD.

Photo by Robert Altman/Michael Ochs Archives/Getty Images

Photo by Archive Photos/Getty Images

artwork that adorns many Mountain albums. On April 17, 1983, at their fifth-floor East Side apartment, she fired a fatal gunshot into Felix's neck. He had given the gun to her for protection. She shot him dead for cheating on her. She claimed it was accidental and was acquitted by a jury of murder but found guilty of criminally negligent homicide, and sentenced to four years in jail, serving only two. By 1983, the stardust had worn off Felix Pappalardi's '60s stardom. He was but a drug-addled ex-rock star with an open marriage. Or so he thought. Gail served her 24 months and left the country for Mexico where she lived under an assumed name before her death from cancer in 2013 at the age of 72.

Earlier in the day, back at the Holiday Inn, Jefferson Airplane loaded up their equipment in a Ford LTD Station Wagon, found an access road for tractors and slowly crawled in (they would crawl out the same way). They felt bad about brushing up against the side of some abandoned cars, scraping off paint jobs, causing small fender benders but, hell, they had to get there! Going onstage 11 hours late frazzled their nerves backstage, especially when they talked amongst themselves about getting to the next gig of the tour.

Jefferson Airplane bassist Jack Casady: "We were totally exhausted. But we were young. When you're young, you can go three days without sleep no problem. No musician back in the day

As Grace Slick (left) put it, Jefferson Airplane played the "morning maniac music" slot when they took the stage Sunday morning.

liked playing outdoors. You just couldn't get the right sound back then outside. You've got the wind playing havoc with the kind of P.A. system that was nothing like today...the ability to carry sound over a great distance...the ability to keep your guitar in tune...the fear of getting electrocuted on stage with all the rain, knowing our onstage stuff couldn't possibly be properly grounded. Nowadays, of course, everything is a lot different. But back then, people were just doing it and nobody had a blueprint for putting on Woodstock. It was learn as you go."

Jefferson Airplane singer/songwriter/ guitarist Paul Kantner (to Michael Lang in *The Road To Woodstock*): "We always liked to go into water of untested depth, so we went to Woodstock with open minds. And it was fucked up, which was good. If it would have been completely organized, then it would have really been fucked up. But the sense of chaos and anarchy—two of my favorite words—prevailed and made it as it was. No fences, no security, none of that shit."

Jack Casady: "By the time we went on, the drugs wore off. Prior to going on, though, we were having a great old time just like everyone else. We all loved Richie Havens, Santana and Ravi Shankar. There was a lot of time hanging out right on the stage, in the wings, waiting for something to happen. All the rain and equipment delays were rather dramatic. Don't forget, that stage was an innovation in and of itself. It was on a platform, an engine-motor platform, shaped like a big circle with half the circle facing the audience and the other half being set up for the next act while one band played. The plan was for the

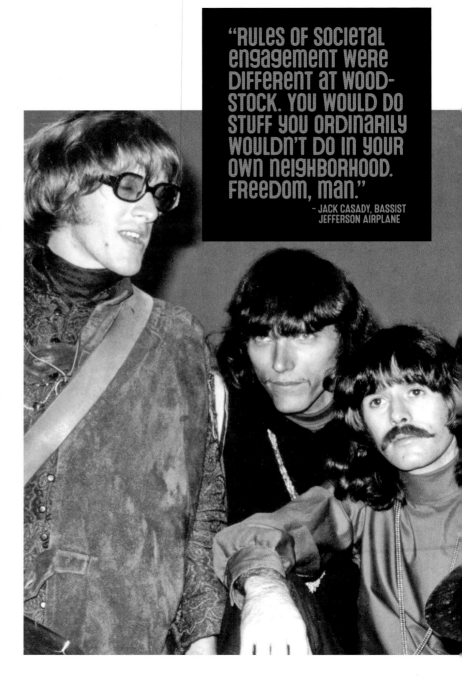

"RULES OF SOCIETAL ENGAGEMENT WERE DIFFERENT AT WOODSTOCK. YOU WOULD DO STUFF YOU ORDINARILY WOULDN'T DO IN YOUR OWN NEIGHBORHOOD. FREEDOM, MAN."

– JACK CASADY, BASSIST
JEFFERSON AIRPLANE

For Jefferson Airplane, the darlings of the San Francisco psychedelic rock scene, Woodstock "was a wide-eyed thrill."

Michael Ochs Archives/Getty Images

stage to circle around so the next band could begin and the process would start over again. Of course, it didn't work, so none of that happened. The production guys were running around like crazy just to get everything up and running and working. Nothing like this had ever been done before."

Paul Kantner: "I got high on acid, walked around, hung out. People were setting up tents and campfires, cooking, swimming and dancing. It was a like a children's crusade, a great social experiment. It simply hadn't happened before. It was akin to whitewater rafting in that you never know what's around the next bend and you're not even worried about it because you're too busy pushing yourself off the rocks."

Jack Casady: "We knew this was different. It was a wide-eyed thrill for us all, like Alice jumping through the rabbit hole where, uh, one pill makes you larger, so to speak, and one pill makes you small. ... Everybody was thrown into the mud pit. Musicians included. We certainly were not prepared for what actually took place at Woodstock. Audiences were a little looser in those days. You pay so much money for a damn ticket nowadays; you have a right to expect nothing but the best sound, lights, presentation. It's almost like fans today don't want surprises. They know what they're going to see and they want it just right. The presentation overshadows the music these days. Everyone wants a spectacular show. An event! Like half-time at The Super Bowl. At Woodstock, people just wanted the music. Needed the music. There was no fancy lighting or staging. The musicians were there to be heard and seen and I don't think anybody cared about presentation. Only the music counted."

Janis Joplin casually strolled on to the Woodstock stage at 2:00 in the morning.

"How are you all? I mean, man, how are you out there? Are you ok? You staying stoned? You got enough water? You got a place to sleep? I don't mean to be preachy but the music's for grooving, man. It's not for putting yourself through bad changes. You don't have to take anybody's shit just to like the music, man. You know what I mean? You don't. You really don't. So if you're getting more shit than you deserve, you know what to do about it, man, you know you gotta try just a little bit harder."

And with that introduction, Joplin kick-started her band into "Try (Just A Little Bit Harder)." It wasn't her usual intro to that song. There was one night, at The Stanley Theater in Jersey City, New Jersey, that was snowing so heavily, hardly anybody showed up. I snuck down front to the very first row because of all the empty seats, as did dozens of others before the cops sent us back to where we belonged. Janis wouldn't have that.

"You pigs better let the people up front or I'm leaving."

One of the more burly cops (hell, they weren't even real cops, they were rent-a-cops) got upset at being called a pig and climbed on stage to confront her. That's when she hauled off and slugged him, sealing a place in my heart forever.

There was no fighting at Woodstock. But Janis was piss-pants drunk. Or tripping her brains out. Or on heroin. But

Three concertgoers embrace the good vibes at Woodstock.

A young music lover enjoys some monkey business while waiting for the next band to play.

Stripped of societal constraints, a Woodstock reveler seeks new heights of freedom.

Photo by Archive Photos/Getty Images

she soldiered on. She had been soldiering on ever since she was practically kicked out of her Texas hometown, blowing out her voice before her first album was even released.

She was the ultimate hippie hero, an overweight, pimpled, insecure girl, not pretty, scorned throughout high school, made fun of, bullied, ridiculed and branded as an outcast, an oddball. To know Janis, you have to understand that town, Port Arthur, Texas, a stifling, ultraconservative hellhole of a town where the mosquitos are an inch long and if you didn't conform, you were railroaded into the role of troublemaker. Janis was miserable there, turned inward, painted, sang folk and blues songs, and finally found some like-minded

souls whom she'd sit atop the town's big water tower with while listening to Bessie Smith on a portable record player, reading Jack Kerouac books out loud, all the while smoking cigarettes, drinking hooch and dreaming of one day leaving.

When she hit San Francisco and joined Big Brother & The Holding Company, it would be an understatement to say she blossomed. According to the Clive Davis autobiography, *The Soundtrack To My Life*, upon being signed to Columbia Records, Joplin bluntly asked Davis, then the president of Columbia, "do you wanna ball?" The book quotes manager Albert Grossman, who confirmed the story, as explaining that just signing a piece of paper was too corporate an act for Janis. She really did want to cement her burgeoning relationship with Columbia Records by having sex with its president. That would make it more personal and less corporate. Davis, although he took it as the supreme complement, turned Janis down.

Bill Graham in his autobiography *Bill Graham Presents: My Life Inside Rock and Out*: "Janis Joplin's talent was that you believed she was singing her guts out every night. You were watching a candle burn, with no wax to replace what had already been used

Bill Hanley, known as the "father of festival sound," works his craft among the assembled as sound engineer at Woodstock.

Photo by Ralph Ackerman/Getty Images

Some people got high for the experience while others got high for the view.

Photo by Three Lions/Getty Images

up. Janis was a feel, an emotion, a spur. Janis was not a song. Janis was the first white singer of that era who sounded like she had come from the world of black blues. I don't think men found her that attractive. I think men found her an awesome female. Not necessarily sexually but sensually. She aroused something in men. She aroused desire but was not the object of that desire. And I think she was never able to deal with that reality."

Janis Joplin: "I don't sleep. That's the trouble. I got to get some damn sleep sometime, I know. But there's so much happening, man. Why sleep? I might miss a party."

"WE DROVE UP FRIDAY FROM ALLENTOWN, PENNSYLVANIA, TOOK US EIGHT HOURS. MUDDY, HUNGRY AND BURNT, WE LEFT SATURDAY AFTER JEFFERSON AIRPLANE. POSITIONED UNDER THE TOWERS, WE CLIMBED UP AND UP AND STAYED REALLY HIGH UP IN THE AIR WITH A GREAT VIEW UNTIL THEY TOLD US FROM THE STAGE TO GET OFF THE TOWERS. BEING GOOD JEWISH BOYS, WE LISTENED, AND CAME RIGHT DOWN."

– ROB FREEMAN, NOW A BUSINESSMAN IN HOLLYWOOD, FLORIDA, WAS 17 WHEN HE WENT TO WOODSTOCK.

Creedence drummer Doug Clifford: "When Janis was singing [at Woodstock], we were trying like hell to get out of there. We had another gig in New Jersey the next night so we were forced to put our business hats on and leave the garden. We knew it would be great to stay and hang with Janis when she finished because, above all, Janis loved Creedence. She was yet another Bay Area musician and whenever we were playing at the Fillmore West, if she wasn't workin', she'd be there. How many times was she in our dressing room drinking her Southern Comfort? She would say, 'I just love y'all. You ain't one of those psychedelic bands, you the real shit, man!' That's what she said to us on more than one occasion. We'd go, 'same to you, sweetheart. We love you too and you're the real shit as well!' We didn't like that psychedelic stuff either. But we were told not to get too close to her. It was for the best not to."

A little more than a year after playing Woodstock, Janis Joplin was in L.A. with her new band, Full Tilt Boogie, recording what would be her most successful album, *Pearl*. She didn't get to see the album completed. Janis was found dead from an accidental heroin overdose in her room at the Landmark Motor Hotel in Hollywood. She was 27. It was Sunday, October 4, 1970, about two weeks after the death of Jimi Hendrix.

> "I don't sleep. That's the trouble. I got to get some damn sleep sometime, I know. But there's so much happening, man. Why sleep? I might miss a party."
> — JANIS JOPLIN

Photo by David Fenton/Getty Images

Photo by Daily Mirror/Mirrorpix/Mirrorpix via Getty Images

Janis Joplin's star rose fast and burned bright. Sadly, it burned out just as quickly. She was dead at 27.

they're playing our song

om Law led yoga exercises from the stage in-between bands. The part-time Hog Farmer realized the political implications of such an event but downplayed them to author Joel Makower in the 1989 book *Woodstock: The Oral History*: "On the first day, there was a bunch of political groups there and they all came to try to make their statements, but they realized...that this wasn't the time for that. It was a time to prove your philosophy, not to talk about it. And if people were resisting the war and wanted peace, well, then, act peacefully. And they did."

And yet the concern that something could go awfully wrong was felt by fan Scott Stoner:

"When I saw the military helicopters, I got really paranoid that the devious Nixon Administration had gathered all the Northeast hippies in one spot for a nefarious reason. That thought crossed my mind more than once."

Activist Abbie Hoffman never met a microphone he didn't like, until he foolheartedly approached Pete Townshend's mic at Woodstock.

David Fenton/Getty Images

> # "I KNOW IT'S CLICHÉ TO SAY WE WITNESSED THE SOUNDTRACK TO OUR LIVES BUT, MAN, THERE IT WAS. RIGHT BEFORE US. LIVE. IN THE MOMENT."
> – NEIL YEAGER

Political activist Abbie Hoffman, who was a huge help in the medical tent talking people down off bad trips, told author Makower in his book that "Woodstock could have turned into the tragedy that Rockefeller had envisioned so easily...It could have been...a thousand dead just from panicking, from bad information or, you know, 'someone's got a knife, run!' ...You could have seen thirty thousand people start to stampede up a hill. I mean, very bad. Especially in the nighttime."

Hoffman's worst fears never materialized. Even so, he played a critical role in one of the more memorable confrontations to come out of the weekend. Here's what Stoner – who had made his way to the front of the stage – recalls of the surreal dustup between Hoffman and Pete Townshend of The Who.

Pete Townshend of The Who wasn't buying into the whole peace-and-love scene at Woodstock, which Abbie Hoffman discovered firsthand.

Monitor Picture Library/Photoshot/Getty Images

Stoner: "My clearest recollection of the whole weekend was watching [The Who] and sensing how pissed off they seemed to be. Maybe that's why the punks always loved them a generation later when punk rock went to war against the whole concept of rock stars. Man, they were great. But Townshend was just so intense. It was like he didn't want to be there.

Michael Lang (from his book): "Since Pete Townshend arrived [at Woodstock], he's been scowling at everyone and keeping to himself. This peace 'n' love thing isn't for him!"

Which probably explains what happened between two of the biggest personalities of the Sixties.

Stoner: "[Towhshend] stepped back away from his microphone to do a solo and—all of a sudden—there's this guy, coming up and standing at Pete's microphone. I didn't know it was Abbie Hoffman. He had been on the stage in the wings. He starts yelling this political rap into Townshend's mic about the manager of Detroit rock band MC5, John Sinclair, and how he was rotting in jail over two joints. Townshend looks up, and now I'm fascinated by this onstage drama unfolding right in front of me, and I'm SO close, and I see Townshend just walk up behind Hoffman, he pulls back the guitar, got his left hand on the

While things heated up on stage, kids sought to cool off with fresh water delivered by tanker trucks to the festival grounds.

neck, his right hand on the body and just brings it around and whacks Hoffman right across the right temple with the head stock of his guitar. Hoffman crumbles and rolls off to the side.

"Townshend steps back up to the mic, looks around to both sides of the stage, and says, 'the next fucking person who walks across this stage is going to get fucking killed!' People started laughing and clapping until Townshend scowls at them again and says, 'you can laugh but I mean it!' Now people in the front start going, 'hey, peace, man, peace!' Townshend looks at them and says, 'I can dig it.' Now the sun's coming up behind [Roger] Daltrey and it's just so spectacular. But the vibe had changed. Now things seemed tense. And I think it added to their encore of 'My Generation.'"

The Who was a tough act to follow, which might explain why Jefferson Airplane struggled so to capture the audience. "By the time Grace Slick walked onstage, I was tired, worn-out, and, I must admit, Jefferson Airplane left me cold," Stoner says. "The crowd seemed to be ignoring them."

Neil Yeager: "I remember sleeping through most of Jefferson Airplane who kept waking me up. It was so physically uncomfortable, though. The music had to keep us in its thrall and it did. It was the only thing we had. We didn't really care about the uncomfortable conditions because the music just transcended that.

"All the other stuff was kind of inconsequential to what was happening on the stage. I know it's cliché to say we witnessed the soundtrack to our lives

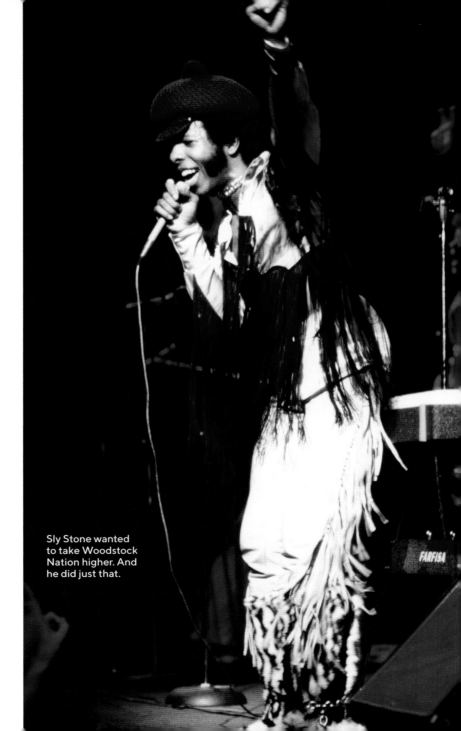

Sly Stone wanted to take Woodstock Nation higher. And he did just that.

but, man, there it was. Right before us. Live. In the moment. We didn't over-think it. We just drank it in. And it stayed with us the rest of our lives. Music has been so central to my life, gotten me through some very dark times. And that music, on that weekend, it was like, 'here's your life. Playing out in front of you in ways unimaginable and inconceivable.' So it didn't matter how difficult or hard the conditions were, how hungry, cold, wet or thirsty you were, the music had the power to transport you.

"Imagine being at a concert now and being thirsty or having to pee? You leave and come back. Without a second thought. I remember the ethos of being in that moment, and the sense that eventually I did realize how magical, unreal and dream-like it was. I remember thinking, 'if people only knew.' Funny thing but people did know because when I got back, my friends said, 'I can't believe you were there. I wish I would've gone!'"

Sly Stone looked out at the living, breathing creature that nestled in the dark right in front of him. It was like the fantasmagoria of a psychedelic pinwheel. So he said the following: "What we would like to do is sing a song together. Now, you see what usually happens is you get a group of people that might sing, and for some reasons that are not unknown anymore, they won't do it. Most of us need approval. Most of us need to get approval from our neighbors before we can actually let it all hang down, you dig? What is happening here is we're gonna try and do a singalong. But a lot of people don't like to do it because they feel that it might be old-fashioned. But you must dig that it is not a fashion in the first place. It is a feeling...and if it was good in the past, it's still good. We would like to sing a song called 'Higher' and if we can get everybody to join in, we'd appreciate it. Everybody please do what you can for me."

The set by Sly & The Family Stone not only exceeded all possible expectations, it transcended Woodstock into Funk Church. "Call and Response" has traditionally been the domain of the religious. When Sly asked us to shout out "higher" and a whole city rose as one and yelled it into the black night air sometime between 3:00 and 4:00 in the morning, then again, then again. it galvanized a generation. Most of us, certainly not I, had ever seen such an act! Their sound, especially with those slide-pump horns, slap-bottom bass of Larry Graham, shrieking lead guitar of Freddie Stone and the charismatic powers—man, he was at the top of his game—of Sly, made Janis Joplin's new band, which he followed, sound like a bunch of amateurs.

But he wasn't finished. He was the High Priest who wanted to take us even higher.

"Get up off your feet and say 'Higher!' and throw the peace sign up! It'll do you no harm. Still, again, some people feel that they shouldn't because there are situations where you need approval to get in on something that could do you some good. Wanna take you higher: Higher! So if you throw the peace sign up and say 'Higher,' everybody'll do it... There's a whole lotta people here and a whole lotta people might not wanna do it because they feel that they can some-how get around it and feel that there are enough people to make up for it and on and on, et cetera, et cetera. We're gonna try 'higher' again and if we can get everybody to join in, we'd appreciate it. It can do you no harm. Wanna take you higher: Higher! Way up there on the hill. Wanna take you higher: Higher! Wanna take you higher: Higher! Wanna take you higher: Higher!"

Former Sly & The Family Stone bass-ist Larry Graham: in 1977: "I remember playing and not being able to see the audience. I heard them and felt them, though. And when that happened we sorta went into overdrive and, uh, I guess, everybody liked it."

What most people don't know is that John Morris, who booked the band, had to practically get physical with the diva rock star Sly who sat and refused to go on as a city waited in the dark. Almost impossible to deal with on any business level, Sly was using one of the trailers as his own personal dressing room. Morris, who had worked for Bill Graham at the Fillmore East, learned from The Master, and put what he learned into effect when he grabbed Sly with two fistfuls of the star's ruffled shirt, lifting him up in the air and informing him in no uncertain terms that he would, indeed, get the hell out on the stage NOW. And he did.

Scott Stoner was having his own prob-lems Sunday of a different sort.

"I was pretty much alone all day Sunday. To get back to the site, you had to cross a main road that had draining ditches running along the sides. There were boards put across the draining ditches so you could walk across from the road to the field. I slipped off the board with my right leg and went into this muck which totally swallowed up my sandal. It just sucked it away. When I put my foot back down, I couldn't seem to feel for it so I just threw my other sandal into the drainage ditch and went barefoot for the rest of the day. This proved unfortunate as a couple hours later, I stepped into some broken glass. My foot was bleeding profusely and it got to be a real problem but I found the medical tent. They were very efficient with a great bedside manner. They cleaned it up, wrapped it up and gave me a plastic baggie to put over the wrap and I even think they gave me a tetanus shot."

Woodstock might have turned out different without the aesthetic of The Hog Farm—who got their name when they first started out by babysitting pigs. They ran the campgrounds, the medical tent and the free kitchen. Flown over from New Mexico, they had been at it already for four years. Hugh Romney, later known as Wavy Gravy, is a hippie hero who knew there was honor in playing the clown.

Ralph Ackerman/Getty Images

The Hog Farm Collective, led by Hugh "Wavy Gravy" Romney, supplemented the overrun concession stands, serving brown rice and vegetables and, more famously, granola.

A brilliant manipulator, Romney calmed down freaked-out LSD trippers, fed people, coddled people, made people laugh, and became an important presence, much more than anybody could have envisioned. He was, and is, a poet and a prophet who, early in his career, used to open shows for John Coltrane and Thelonious Monk with his stand-up comedy and beat poetry, and was managed for a short time by Lenny Bruce. His wife Bonnie Jean was immortalized by Bob Dylan when he wrote a song about her called "Girl From The North Country." Other Hog Farmers included members of Ken Kesey's Merry Pranksters (immortalized in Tom Wolfe's *The Electric Kool-Aid Acid Test*).

"So now I'm lugging around this cut foot which was aching," remembers Stoner. "I didn't pay any attention to Joe Cocker until the one song I knew, 'With A Little Help From My Friends' and it was great. I got a little nervous when the rains came. My foot was killing me, there was no music, the rain kept getting harder and harder. I just stood around watching people slide in the mud. When the rain finally ended, I was soaked, and very cold. People were building fires. A lot of people had left with the rain. I got warm next to a fire built by people who didn't mind me sharing their space at all. I wound up lying down by that fire, trying to keep warm and dozing off. I awoke for Crosby, Stills, Nash & Young but my foot was really throbbing.

"I stuck around for half of Paul Butterfield's set before starting my painful hike back to the cars. They were all there. It was Monday morning and the sun was shining again. We debated the relative merits of waiting for Hendrix but I was in too much pain and they were all really tired. My last recollection was hearing the oddly-placed 'Duke Of Earl.' I knew Gene Chandler wasn't on the bill and I was mystified who'd be playing that oddball doo-wop song at Woodstock. I found out later 'Duke Of Earl' and 'Get A Job' were the last two songs by Sha Na Na. That meant I was only two songs away from seeing Hendrix."

The third day of the festival was memorable for yet another reason. Early Sunday afternoon, Max Yasgur, the dairy farmer who gave of his land, risking his reputation in the community and his livelihood, addressed the Woodstock crowd:

Woodstock staff were given two T-shirts: red for security and medical team members; and blue for stage crew.

"I'm a farmer. I don't know how to speak to 20 people at one time, let alone a crowd like this. But I think you people have proven something to the world. Not only to the town of Bethel or Sullivan County or New York State. You've proven something to the world. This is the largest group of people ever assembled in one place. We have had no idea that there would be this size group and because of that, you had quite a few inconveniences as far as water and food and so forth. Your producers have done a mammoth job to see that you're taken care of. They'd enjoy a vote of thanks.

"But above that, the important thing that you've proven to the world is that a half a million kids, and I call you kids because I have children older than you, a half million young people can get together and have three days of fun and music and have nothing but fun and music. And God bless you for it."

Max became a hero to us all and I cannot listen to that speech today without a tear. He owned the land upon which we grooved and smoked and loved and slept. The nearby town of Wallkill didn't want us. With days to go and no site, he stepped up and didn't care how long our hair was, or that we'd be smoking massive amounts of pot on his property. He went to bat for us with the town fathers in Bethel.

At the zoning ordinance meeting with local politicos, Max, a lifelong Republican, said the following. "I hear you are considering changing the zoning law to prevent the festival. I hear you don't like the look of the kids who are working at the site. I hear you don't like their

Max Yasgur, the dairy farmer turned Woodstock hero.

Bill Eppridge/The LIFE Picture Collection/Getty Images

Max Yasgur was one of the largest milk producers in Sullivan County, New York. His farm had 650 cows, mostly Guernseys.

I'm going back to running a dairy farm." And he did. But the abuse kept coming—he wasn't exactly a healthy man at the time—and it was that abuse, in part, that made him sell the farm in 1971 and move to Florida where he suffered a fatal heart attack in 1973 at the age of 53. God bless him.

The youngest person on that stage all weekend was Sha Na Na lead guitarist Henry Gross, who was barely 18. "I was too young to be scared," Gross says. "I remember touring with Van Morrison and he said he was always scared prior to and always nervous while performing. Others far more well known than myself

lifestyle. I hear you don't like they are against the war and that they say so very loudly... I don't particularly like the looks of some of those kids either. I don't particularly like their lifestyle, especially the drugs and free love. And I don't like what some of them are saying about our government. However, if I know my American history, tens of thousands of Americans in uniform gave their lives in war after war just so those kids would have the freedom to do exactly what they are doing. That's what this country is all about and I am not going to let you throw them out of our town just because you don't like their dress or their hair or the way they live or what they believe. This is America and they are going to have their festival."

He stood his ground when locals wanted to boycott his dairy farm and not buy his milk. He showed up day after day at Woodstock with eggs and bread for the kids. He didn't want to speak on stage. It just wasn't in his nature. He had to be forced into making that statement by being told that the fans really needed to see who the man was that kept the festival and the Woodstock spirit alive. So he spoke.

After the festival, the locals shunned him. His own neighbors turned their backs on him. The general store wouldn't accept his goods. This just made him even more resolute, although he did turn down a request to have a similar concert on his property again in 1970, saying, "as far as I know,

Despite the fears of locals, law enforcement was impressed by the behavior of Woodstock Nation.

have said the same thing. The only thing that ever made me nervous in the music industry was if the check would bounce."

Sha Na Na was an odd fit for Woodstock. The band was a throwback to an earlier era. It was an act more suited for the Broadway stage than Woodstock. It was 7:30 Monday morning by the time they went into their choreographed routine of songs from the 1950s. They stuck out like a sore thumb.

"We did the greatest songs of an era that morning," remembers Gross. "Sha Na Na wasn't put together as a real band. It was a glee club from Columbia University, a social club, really, who sang songs like 'Little Darling.' I was a student at Brooklyn College but was in a band singing folk songs in Greenwich Village. I joined them and the group survived on charm. We had an idea and the power of that idea was unstoppable. Sha Na Na spawned the *Happy Days* TV show and the musical *Grease*, bringing original doo-wop rock 'n' roll back from the dead in an era of psychedelia. So why aren't we in the Rock and Roll Hall of Fame? We changed the face of music for at least a little while. In the same way that The Blues Brothers brought back big-time Chicago blues like Muddy Waters and Howling Wolf, Sha Na Na brought back Chuck Berry, Bill Haley and all those vocal groups who got a big boost from what we did.

"Sha Na Na had no competition there. Doo-wop music was what we all

Unlike any other act at Woodstock, Sha Na Na covered 1950s pop and doo-wop standards.

Henry Gross was barely 18 when he performed with Sha Na Na at Woodstock. As a solo artist, he scored a hit single with the song "Shannon."

loved growing up. I was glued to it. I was poised to be a founding member of Sha Na Na. So to me, Woodstock was just another gig. Every show we ever did went down great."

Hendrix followed Sha Na Na to close Woodstock. There could not have been a greater contrast. Or so it would seem.

"Jimi loved Sha Na Na and would always come out to see us when we played Steve Paul's Scene in midtown Manhattan on 46th Street," Gross says. "Steve managed Johnny and Edgar Winter. Man, we blew that place up! Eric Clapton came down and jammed with us. Rick Derringer too. We did shows with Dr. John and Slim Harpo. It was a great time to be alive in New York City.

"Jimi was an amazing guy, just wonderful, a real sweetheart. Once we were jamming at The Scene. The dressing room was underneath the staircase. I was sitting in there and in walks Jimi with his guitar case. We immediately start talking when this guy comes in trying to sell us a Nikon camera. He was obviously a drug addict who had just stolen it. 'How much you want for it,' Jimi asked. '$200.' Jimi goes into his pocket, pulls out $200 cash and gives it to the guy who gives Jimi the camera. He puts it down, forgets about it, and

we do our thing, just talking while people are coming in and out. When we left, at about 6:00 in the morning after talking and jamming all night, Jimi puts his guitar back in the case and heads for the stairwell. 'Hey, you forgot the camera,' I reminded him. 'You keep it,' he told me. He didn't even want it! He just wanted to give the guy some money. That's a small example of his good-hearted nature."

Country Joe McDonald came to Woodstock as part of a band. He left as a solo act.

"There are two perceptions of a performer on stage. One is what the performer onstage is going through. The other one is what the audience is seeing and enjoying," McDonald says. "You can be onstage having a lousy time while thinking about something completely different than what you're singing about. I used to think that the audience somehow knew what I thinking onstage but that's not the case.

"I had arrived on Thursday. I was there pretty much from Richie Havens on. I was at that Holiday Inn with everybody else. I had transport back and forth very easily by finding stage crew guys to drive me. I was enjoying all the acts and having a real good time but by the time Country Joe and the Fish were supposed to go on Sunday, people were chanting 'No Rain! No Rain!' We then had to postpone our performance. At that point, I was like 'fuck this shit! This is horrible!' But we did our Sunday show.

"By a performance standard, it wasn't really that great. We had new members in the band. Three of the original members had either quit, were forced out or

Despite rumors that the National Guard might be sent in to clear out the festival grounds, kids remained laid back.

were fired. I had nothing to do with that. They just disappeared. The drummer quit three weeks before Woodstock with no way of knowing we were going to play. We only got added to the bill two weeks prior.

"I wasn't happy anymore with the band. We had bastardized our own music. We weren't playing our classic material from the first two albums, which was very difficult to play. We only had a few weeks to rehearse with a new drummer, new bass player and new keyboard player, all of whom had been picked by [guitarist] Barry Melton and our manager. I was uncomfortable with them. What had started out fun and happy had soured. The honeymoon period was over, and it quickly fell completely apart at a time when we were at our so-called height. So in addition to the weather, and the personality clashes with myself and Barry, we still went out there, did our thing and gave it our best, or at least the best we could do under the conditions."

McDonald wasn't the only one struggling to come to grips with things on Sunday.

Just as we didn't know on Saturday how close the Governor was to sending in the National Guard to clear us all out, we also didn't know that on Sunday, after the rains came, we were sitting on a minefield of potential disaster. In 2009, John Roberts told Pete Fornatale in *Back To The Garden*: "...when the heavy rains came on Sunday, we got a call from John Morris who said, 'we're a little worried here. We buried the power cables running to the stage under the crowd areas.' We buried them pretty deeply, but with the rain and the masses of people there, they were worried that the dirt was wearing away, and there might be some erosion.

"What they wanted to do was shut the power from those cables to the side and bring the power in some other way. And I said, 'well, what's the practical effect?' He said, 'we'll have to stop the show for a little while, but if we don't and those cables wear through and fray and all those people are wet and packed together—we could have the largest mass electrocution in the history of the world.' So I said, 'well, the answer is pretty obvious. Let's stop the show for a while and do what we have to do to make sure that it's safe.' And that was a pretty nerve-wracking hour. I think that was the single, scariest moment for me."

John Morris: "That was scary, alright. The storm that came through Sunday was, in fact, a tornado. The power lines were, indeed, buried under the audience. There certainly was the possibility of soil erosion exposing the lines and with people wet and huddled together, who knows what might have happened? We were not willing to take that chance so we stopped the show. We explained to the audience that we were going to go off-power for awhile but we'd be back and everything would be okay. Our electricians took care of everything and the audience didn't fry. I'm not sure that they would've but

we didn't want to take the chance."

When the heavy rains hit it was Morris who calmly reassured us all.

"Wrap yourself up, gang," Morris said from the stage. "Looks like we've got to ride this out!"

What else could he have said? But he said it so forthrightly and bluntly that it came as a balm to our savaged souls. When Morris tried to calm us down, he kept getting shocks from the microphone, but the tower climbers listened to him as he told them to get down NOW. And our behavior during survival-like conditions showed the world our peace 'n' love credentials weren't just empty words. We proved it that weekend.

The electrocution scenario was real, Chris Langhart says, but a bit overstated. "Don't forget we're talking about low mobile cables, low being 110 volts that go out to the towers on the right and left of the stage," Langhart says. "These are not the high-voltage cables from the power company, though, which is a totally different thing. Had the power company's 2,400- or 3,200-volt cables been underground, that would have caused a catastrophic problem had those cables become exposed...but all that wiring was overhead.

"I would say that it could have been a problem but, at the time, I didn't consider it a very big problem because 110-volt cables buried in mud that's so close to ground, even if they frayed, would not have caused any major health problems. I mean, sure, you would've felt a tingle on the ground but it certainly wouldn't have mass-electrocuted anybody."

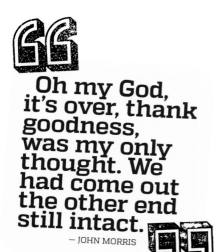

> ## Oh my God, it's over, thank goodness, was my only thought. We had come out the other end still intact.
> — JOHN MORRIS

John Morris: "Right around the same time, I was also told that Joan Baez had suffered a miscarriage, my dog was missing and my wife broke her ankle. Only the last thing was true. I was underneath the stage already stressed about the weather. I climbed up on stage and looked skyward. We had these gigantic trusses above us which I feared would come crashing down on the stage. I would say it was as close to a nervous breakdown as I'd ever came. [Woodstock film Director] Mike Wadleigh was down on one knee with a camera right in front of me filming me during that period because everyone else was off the stage. Hey, those were the problems and that was exactly how strained I felt. And the microphone kept giving me electric shocks. Everything was wet."

Morris couldn't rest easy until Monday. There was too much to worry about. "I didn't let out a sigh of relief until Jimi Hendrix woke me out of sound sleep with the National Anthem. That's when I knew it was finally over and we had pulled it off. We had pushed it and pushed it and had everybody play as long as we could because if we played through, people wouldn't all hit the roads at the same time in darkness. We were wrong. They mostly all left anyway, leaving Jimi to play for a few stragglers Monday morning—maybe 30,00 out of the half-million—and a lot of garbage. It looked like Armageddon out there when Jimi played.

"I got Jimi on stage and went back to my trailer. Went to rest for a brief period and went out like a light, falling into a deep sleep for the first time since Thursday night. Next thing I knew I was hearing 'The Star-Spangled Banner.' I jumped up and out of the trailer and was blinded by the sun. 'Oh my God, it's over, thank goodness,' was my only thought. We had come out the other end still intact. I went for a walk around the site. Three hours later I was still walking. I was looking to see if anyone was out there seriously injured, in trouble or dead. It looked like something that a Civil War photographer might have captured on film. I just kept walking and walking. We were lucky. No one needed any help. There was not one case—zero—of physical violence from one person to another. Amazing."

A man and a child stroll past a cat and people in sleeping bags at Woodstock.

Photo by Ralph Ackerman/Getty Images

Photo courtesy of Kathy and Butch Dukes

Photo courtesy of Kathy and Butch Dukes

Dear Kathy and Butch,

Your letter has been most gratifying. Thank you for writing.

I hope things work out well for you and join in your hope for peace and happiness.

Sincerely,
Max Yasgur

Kathy and Butch Dukes met at Woodstock. Fifty years later they're still enjoying music together.

After Woodstock, Kathy and Butch sent a thank you note to Max Yasgur, who in return wished them "peace and happiness."

A First Date to Remember

By Paul Kennedy

All couples have first dates; some are simply more memorable than others. Meet Kathy and Butch Dukes of North Myrtle Beach, South Carolina, who pretty much have cornered the market on memorable first dates.

"People will meet us and ask 'How can you be so liberal?'" Kathy, 71, says with the amused voice of a woman who gets that question a lot. "I tell them, 'Come on, we met at Woodstock.'"

In the organized chaos that was Woodstock, these two kids crossed paths. Little did they know that they would then share the same path for the next 50 years. "We had fun together and decided to continue the romance," says Butch, 69.

Kathy was 21 in 1969, living in New York's Greenwich Village. Eddie Bigler, a friend living across the hall in her apartment building, suggested they go to this musical festival he had been hearing so much about. So, sleeping bags in hand, Eddie and Kathy headed out. Once on the Woodstock grounds, Eddie bumped into Butch, an old friend. After introductions, Eddie split. Kathy and Butch stayed.

The two found themselves center stage and up the hill, right in the middle of the biggest concert in history. And that's where they stayed, surrounded by hundreds of thousands of people, talking, listening to music and, like all couples on a first date, getting to know each other. "We didn't budge," Kathy says. "Once you sat down there wasn't anywhere to go."

It was nonstop music for Butch and Kathy. Richie Havens, Ten Years After, Jefferson Airplane, they enjoyed them all. But the most notable act? Had to be Sha Na Na, Kathy says. "It was just so outrageous to see these guys in gold lamé outfits singing doo-wop and dancing around. They were just so fun."

Through thick and thin, the couple hung tight. Searing heat, torrential rain, mud, music miracles and delays; all were taken in stride, buoyed by the wonder of youth. "On our way out," Kathy says, "we literally were walking by the stage when Jimi Hendrix was playing the 'Star-Spangled Banner.'"

Who goes their own way after that? Exactly. Which is why after the festival Butch went home, gathered his belongings and moved to New York to be with Kathy. They were married Thanksgiving weekend, 1969. Their daughter, Jessica, was born the next spring. Her middle name is Satori, named after friend Eddie Bigler's cat.

As for Woodstock itself, Kathy and Butch thought it was grand. Butch still has the denim jacket he wore that weekend; mud stains and all.

"I know it's a cliché," Butch says, "but Woodstock was all about love and peace."

For Kathy and Butch Dukes, it's no cliché. Woodstock will always be about love.

CHAPTER EIGHT

LEAVING YASGUR'S FARM

J ohnny Winter's manager Steve Paul made a huge mistake when his client was tuning up onstage and these kids were running around. As he waited in the wings, one of the kids came up to him and asked, "could we please film Mr. Winter's performance?" Almost as if he was W.C. Fields in a 1930s comedy, he practically said, "get out of here, kids, you're bothering me." Little did he know it was *Woodstock* film director Michael Wadleigh and one of his camera men. And that's why Johnny Winter isn't in the movie.

Thirty-nine years later, after surviving a second manager who robbed him blind and kept him high and onstage so the money would continue to pour in, Winter was a died-in-the-wool blues legend, so white he was black, playing a brand of Texas blues that Blind Lemon Jefferson invented, Lightnin' Hopkins and T-Bone Walker refined and Albert Collins/Freddie King/Stevie Ray Vaughan popularized.

It was 2008 and the Museum at Bethel Woods came calling, asking to film Johnny for one of its myriad of artist testimonials. Johnny, being Johnny, refused to go back to the site so the Museum sent a small film crew to his house in Connecticut. By that time, the guitarist was managed by his good friend/bandmate Paul Nelson. Nelson has to be looked upon as the hero of the Johnny Winter story, successfully extricating Winter from the clutches of former bad deals, weaning him off pills, getting him on a healthy regimen that added years to his life and enabled the living legend to continue to prosper and tour right on up to his death in 2014 on the road in Switzerland at age 70. Nelson picks up the story.

"So I had them come over when I knew he'd be home without telling him. Had I told him, he might have said no. I led the crew in through the storm doors of Johnny's backyard, down

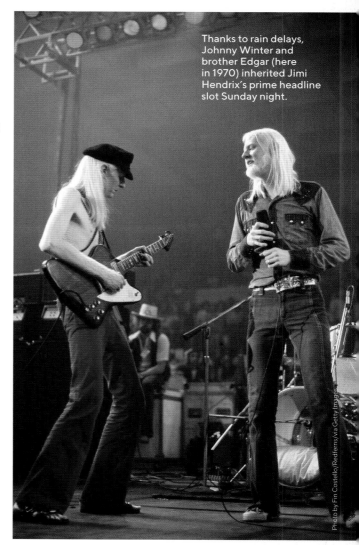

Thanks to rain delays, Johnny Winter and brother Edgar (here in 1970) inherited Jimi Hendrix's prime headline slot Sunday night.

Photo by Fin Costello/Redferns/via Getty Images

into Johnny's basement where they set up. I then went upstairs and impressed upon Johnny that the museum interview represented an opportunity to right the wrong done to him by being excluded from the movie and the original soundtrack. I told him he could finally get the credit he was due. And, oh by the way, I told him they were downstairs in his basement right now all set up to film him.

"'Oh great,' he smiled, and he went down. But when they asked him about Woodstock, he smiled again and simply said, 'I don't remember a thing. I was asleep the whole time I was performing.'

"Nobody knew what to say. How is that even possible? I told the crew to take a time-out, go out for a smoke or

Festival attendees look to catch a ride home as the Woodstock exodus begins.

A misty Sunday sunrise greeted concertgoers on the last day of the festival.

something, and immediately called up his late drummer Uncle John 'Red' Turner and bassist Tommy Shannon. Between the two of them, I was told that, indeed, he was asleep! Apparently, they had been playing plenty of festivals back then and didn't realize at first that Woodstock would be more than just a concert; it would be a movement! So they signed on when asked. The day of the show, the band was picked up by helicopter at Westchester Airport. He fell asleep on the helicopter. They land and pile out to the outside backstage area behind the stage but Johnny is still sleeping so they gently carry him and deposit him from the copter and on to a huge pile of garbage where he remained passed out right next to Jimi Hendrix who was sleeping in a lounge chair. Tommy, Edgar [Winter, Johnny's brother] and Red were so excited that they stayed awake and watched all the artists perform. But Johnny was still out. Dead out.

Edgar Winter: "I was totally asleep on the floor in a press trailer. There was no schedule. It was organized confusion. Plus, a lot of bands were in no condition to play. Folks were running around in a maniacal fever trying to round up anybody who was capable of walking onstage. I was awakened from this deep sleep and desperately told 'we need somebody to go on!' I said I was ready. So were the other guys. I hadn't showered. I had that morning voice. You know that voice when you just wake up? It was the strangest transition from being dead asleep to being so alive on that stage. It was an amazing moment,

Rain ravaged the grounds Sunday afternoon, leaving puddles and mud in its wake.

Bettmann/Getty Images

the impact of which stayed with me for decades... What made it special was its social significance, just the fact that there were so many amazingly talented people on that one stage, so many, in fact, it was magical.

"The cumulative effect of all those great bands in one weekend changed the mindset of a generation. I was there until the very end. We had to push our station wagon through the mud because the helicopters were all gone."

Paul Nelson: "Apparently, from what I can get from the boys, [Johnny] woke up, played, then went back to sleep before being carried back onto the next helicopter out of there. A friend of mine who was there filled me in on everything and even included a missing piece of information about why Hendrix had to play in the morning Monday after most everybody went home. Apparently, after the headlining slot was given to Jimi, Michael Lang came up to him and told him how because of the way the show was going, it would probably be the next morning, Monday, until he ever even would get on. What should be the headlining slot was going to be actually after the concert was over and not really a good slot at all. So the story goes, and this is how it was told to me, Lang told Hendrix if he still wanted to headline in primetime, he could go on at midnight to close the festival, but every act after him wouldn't get to play. He would tell Blood Sweat & Tears, Crosby Stills Nash & Young, Paul Butterfield and Sha Na Na to go home and not play. Hendrix refused on the grounds that he couldn't do

A woman sweeps debris from the street in front of her home in Bethel as music fans leave town.

that to his fellow musicians. That's the kind of guy he was."

Edgar Winter: "I remember the conversations when Johnny's first manager, Steve Paul, who was a very peculiar character, refused to have him in the movie or on the original soundtrack. Sure, it was a huge mistake, but that's only looking at it after the fact. You must remember that at the time nobody had any sense of what Woodstock was or would become. I was there when Steve looked Johnny right in the eye and said, 'boy, whatever you do, don't sign anything. Anything!' Artists were being asked to sign release forms to be in the movie. Steve felt—incorrectly—that Woodstock would be looked back upon in a negative light. He wanted Johnny to distance himself completely from being associated with it because people will eventually forget all about it, but the only thing people forgot—as a direct result of his bad decision—is that Johnny Winter and I performed at Woodstock! It was, I must say, a well-meaning decision. He really did have Johnny's best interests at heart. And there was a lot of negativity coming out of Woodstock. It didn't emerge as iconic immediately. That decision sounds a lot worse in hindsight."

Paul Nelson: "So who do you think got Hendrix's prime headline slot at midnight Sunday night? Johnny Winter! It turned out to be the most attended portion of Woodstock. So I tell all this to Johnny right before his interview with the Woodstock Museum people so he'd have something to say. I was nervous as they were affixing the microphone to his lapel, thinking to myself, wondering if he's going to say any of this. I even had to tell Johnny how muddy it was and I wasn't even born yet during Woodstock. So he looks into the camera—my heart was beating out of my chest—and he says the whole damn story I had just told him about the bag of garbage, the helicopter, Jimi and the mud. Right on cue!"

Edgar Winter: "I wrote 'Dyin' To Live' as a direct result of Woodstock. Most people think of it as an antiwar song but it's much more

Woodstock was all about being in the moment. Few understood the implications of the event at the time.

Campers enjoy one last moment of sunshine before the Sunday afternoon rains arrive.

personal than that. After Woodstock, we lost a lot of our musical heroes. At that time, the whole idea of drugs harbored an innocent enthusiasm. It was all about mind-expansion and the search for self, not to mention freedom. Eventually, it degenerated into people using harder drugs and it became something else altogether. But there was a certain mystique about the whole thing. All my jazz heroes were addicts. In a lot of cases, you thought, 'well, that's what you have to do.' It was sort of a pre-requisite to create. All of that was totally new to me. When it finally sunk in, and I got the idea that it was really a life-threatening thing, that became key in writing 'Dyin' To Live.'"

While brother Johnny couldn't remember anything about Woodstock, Edgar knew the experience changed his life forever.

Edgar Winter: "I was painfully shy as a kid. I'd spend endless hours alone with music. It became my own personal private escape world. Music gave me my sense of identity, a sense of belonging. I never thought about or desired fame. When it got to the actual Woodstock performance, I just will never forget standing on that stage and looking out over this endless sea of humanity. The whole thing was set against the social backdrop of civil rights and the peace movement. That moment, seeing all of those people united in that unique way, is indelibly imprinted in my brain. I'll never forget it. In fact, from that

Waiting for a ride back home, a festivalgoer bides his time playing guitar.

thereafter I recorded my *Entrance* debut and then put together my first band, White Trash. Had it not been for Woodstock, my whole career might never have happened."

In his 1988 autobiography *Long Time Gone*, David Crosby writes of Woodstock, "Woodstock was a time when there was a prevailing feeling of harmony. Was it really an 'Aquarian Festival of Peace and Love and Music'? Hard to answer because I didn't give a damn about Aquarian this or Aquarian that. I think astrology is complete bullshit...

"The other notable thing about Woodstock was that we were scared, as Stephen [Stills] said in the film. What wasn't said in the movie is why we were so nervous: everyone we respected in the whole goddamn music business was

(above) Woodstock organizer Michael Lang had a reason to be pleased: he had pulled off the impossible.

(right) Stephen Stills performs Sunday night as part of Crosby, Stills, Nash & Young.

point forward, I first came to realize that music was not just my own personal private world. It really had the power to reach out, transcend boundaries and bring people together.

"The concept of me actually being an artist formulated inside me for the very first time at Woodstock. It was a direct result of Woodstock that shortly

standing in a circle behind us when we went on. Everybody was curious about us. We were the new kid on the block, it was our second public gig, nobody had ever seen us, everybody had heard the record, everybody wondered, 'what in the hell are they about?' Every band that played there, including all the ones that aren't in the movie, were all standing in an arc behind us, and that was intimidating, to say the least. I'm looking back at Hendrix and Robbie Robertson and Levon Helm and Janis and Sly and Grace and Paul, everyone that I knew and everyone I didn't know. We were so happy that it went down well that we could barely handle it."

Graham Nash, though, had no trouble handling it.

Graham Nash: "Woodstock didn't freak me out at all because I'd already done it. I'd done seven years with The Hollies. Certainly not as big a crowd as that but it was the same fervor. We had girls grabbing our ties trying to rip our clothes off, trying pull our hair out. I'd been through all that. Nothing, even Woodstock, could rattle me after that. To me? It was no big deal. I was pretty chill throughout. Look at the footage. Does that look like a man all freaked out? I was very comfortable on that stage."

Still, the group had major misgivings about the gig. David Geffen had told them about the size of the crowd. That's when Stephen Stills nixed the whole idea. He called John Morris to say that they weren't coming. Morris, who had been putting out fires all weekend, put out another one when he told Stills that he was playing their debut album over the loudspeakers and people were digging it. It did the trick.

Jimi Hendrix, dressed in a white fringed and beaded leather jacket, with a red scarf around his head, looked out upon a sea of garbage and about 30,000 stragglers. Most everybody had already gone home. It was 9:00 Monday

A concertgoer ponders his next move among the debris left behind by Woodstock Nation.

morning when he ambled onstage with an under-rehearsed jam band of friends. Erroneously introduced as "The Jimi Hendrix Experience" (which had broken up), he peered into the sunshine and said, "You can leave if you want to. We're just jamming, that's all. You can leave or you can clap." He had been offered a more primetime slot but wanted to close the show. He was also offered a Friday solo opening acoustic slot but that never happened. Jimi wasn't even Michael Lang's first choice to close the show. Lang wanted Western star Roy Rogers to sing "Happy Trails" and send everybody home on a wistful nostalgic note, but the cowboy turned him down.

In the act of introducing his fellow jammers, Jimi told us, "We got tired of the Experience and every once in a while we were blowing our minds too much, so we decided to change the whole thing around and call it Gypsy, Sun and Rainbows … we only had about two rehearsals, so … nothing but primary-rhythm things, but, I mean, it's a first ray of the new rising sun, anyway, so we might as well start from the earth, which is rhythm, right?" And with that, he launched into "Message To Love."

My friend Neil Yeager had made a promise to call home. I stayed put and he ventured out into the great unknown of the audience.

Neil Yeager: "When we parted on Sunday so I could call our moms, after waiting in line for a few hours, I found some food, a comparatively comfortable place to stay and just listened while you were freaking out about my absence. It's amazing I even found my way back to you! We both individually kept leaving and coming back so we must have drawn the map in our minds as to where we were via the stage because we were so close. I know I had certain reference points so I did what everybody did, just sort of wander around until I found you. Some folks planted flags which made it a little easier. By Sunday, with hardly any sleep, I was rather exhausted. I wanted to leave before you did but I knew we

People soon discovered it was more fun to party than it was to clean up after one.

both had to agree on leaving before we left so I stayed.

"We got totally lost in leaving and I thought we would never find the car. Don't forget, when we got there Thursday, the crowd was still rather sparse but building fast. The site looked different. And with dozens of parking lots housing tens of thousands of cars, it seemed almost impossible to find ours. But we did. In fact, a sense of serene calm overtook the both of us while walking in the dark and feeling so safe like nothing could possibly happen to us. To this day, I associate music with an inner peace and well-being."

Boston Globe, August 19, 1969 Editorial Page: "The Woodstock Music and Art Festival will surely go down in history as a mass event of great and positive significance in the life of the country...That this many young people could assemble so peaceably and with such good humor in a mile-square area...speaks volumes about their dedication to the idea of respect for the dignity of the individual... In a nation beset with a crescendo of violence, this is a vibrantly hopeful sign. If violence is infectious, so, happily, in nonviolence. The benign character of the young people gathered at Bethel communicated itself to many of their elders, including policemen, and the generation gap was successfully bridged in countless cases. Any event which can do this is touched with greatness."

Max Yasgur, in a rare post-concert press conference, told reporters...

"The kids were wonderful, honest, sincere, good kids who said, 'here we are. This is what we are. This is the way

On his way out of town after Woodstock, Michael Lang noticed the people starting the monumental task of cleaning up the site had created a huge peace symbol out of the garbage they were collecting.

Photo by Daniel Wolf/The Boston Globe via Getty Images

we dress. These are our morals.' There wasn't one incident the whole time. The kids were polite, shared everything with everyone, and they forced me to open my eyes. I think America has to take notice. What happened at Bethel this past weekend was that these young people together with our local residents turned the Aquarian festival into a dramatic victory for the spirit of peace, good will and human kindness." To which Sullivan County Sheriff Louis Ratner added, "I never met a nicer bunch of kids in my life."

Graham Nash, at 76, still looks every inch the rock star. His 2013 autobiography, *Wild Tales: A Rock'n'Roll Life*, is among the best of tell-all books. It got him in trouble with David Crosby but that's nothing new. And he doesn't really care. Crosby, Stills, Nash and Young are all still alive but don't expect a reunion. They've already been offered $100 million and turned it down, according to Nash, who says it's not about the money. "We have to like each other to make music."

Fifty years earlier, it was far less complicated. Harmony existed in their music and their lives.

"We heard in June of '69 that Michael Lang was going to put on this big show that his team was pitching as a multi-artist concert for maybe 40,000, if that. We looked at each other and went, 'hmmm, that's an interesting proposition.' Then, as the event got closer and closer, estimates ballooned up to 200,000. After we signed on, we get a call saying there might even be 300,000. It kept getting higher."

Nash and Joni Mitchell were lovers at the time. For that fateful weekend in August, they shared a beautiful suite of rooms which included a grand piano. When Crosby, Stills and Nash finally got back to the suite after performing at Woodstock they find Joni at the piano working on a song. Asked to perform at Woodstock, her manager, Elliot Roberts, nixed the idea, thinking Mitchell wouldn't be able to get back to New York City on time to do "The Dick Cavett Show" which—to be on a national major network program for the first time— was important for her career.

"Elliot realized," explains Nash, "that as it was getting closer to the show, how crazy it was getting with the amount of people who were streaming in blocking all the roadways. He told Joni, 'you'll never get out of there in time to make the Cavett show and we simply cannot take that chance. You've got

Joni Mitchell and Graham Nash at the Big Sur Folk Festival in California, a month after Woodstock.

to be on the TV show.'"

So she spent her time in the suite watching the news about the festival and listening to the radio personalities talk about the festival.

When the boys returned, Mitchell said, "I want to play you something."

"That's when she played 'Woodstock' for us for the very first time," says Nash with a definite twinkle in his eye as he is transported back in time. "She had been soaking it all up and it all came out in that song, despite her having never even having been there."

Graham was all ears. So were Crosby and Stills, who still had his muddy boots on. Neil Young wasn't there. "When she finished, no one said a word. Stills, with his elbows on the piano, was staring intently at her, his eyes glazed over in a dreamy appreciation of what he had just heard," according to Nash.

Stephen Stills: "Hey Joni, uh, could we have that song?"

Joni Mitchell: "What?"

Stephen Stills: "Can the three of us have that song?"

Joni Mitchell: (with no hesitation whatsoever) "Sure, of course you can."

"The song wasn't even complete at the time," Nash softly says with a wistful tone. "She was still writing it. The original way she wrote it, it's hard to explain, but it was kind of more—for want of a

Joni Mitchell didn't play Woodstock, opting instead to go on "The Dick Cavett Show." She did, however, write the best song about the event, and gave it to Crosby, Stills, Nash & Young with no questions asked. Here, Mitchell (center) performs with John Sebastian, Graham Nash, David Crosby and Stephen Stills during the 1969 Big Sur Folk Festival in Big Sur, California.

Photo by Robert Altman/Michael Ochs Archives/Getty Images

better phrase—dark purple. It was in a mysterious kind of minor key. It was slow, slower, definitely darker than what it became in our hands, which was kind of celebratory. Once she said we could have it, Stephen then says, 'do you mind if we change it around a little bit?' He instinctively knew what he wanted to do with it. He knew it had to rock in our hands."

"Go ahead," she told him.

"You've got to understand, Joni loves all three of us. She just loves us. Always has. Don't forget, she was the very first witness to the voices of Crosby, Stills and Nash singing together for the very first time. There were four of us in the room that fateful night at her place: David, Stephen, Joni and myself. She was witness. Stephen says it was Mama Cass Elliot but he's wrong. It was Joni. And I loved Cass. Cass is the reason we're talking right now. I've put her name on every single album we've ever done since she died. But it wasn't Cass. It was Joni Mitchell who first heard us, as we first heard ourselves, in her living room.

"Now, you can't think of that song without Neil Young's giant spider guitar intro. Then Stephen answers him with his own lead in contrast. I must say, Neil Young is one fantastic musician. Not a lot of people even realize he was at Woodstock. He refused to be in the movie. He refused to even be photographed onstage. I don't think Neil thinks even today that was a big mistake on his part. And why should he?

"I know the myth of Woodstock has grown tremendously. But it was a fascinating show in retrospect. I can never undo the experience of Woodstock. It's in me now for good. And I was almost killed getting there. We had a series of helicopters taking us in. I was in one with our drummer Dallas Taylor and Crosby. We're flying over the crowd. That's when David said, 'it looks like

Joe Cocker (onstage) had his hands full with a distracted Sunday afternoon crowd.

an encampment of the Macedonian Army.' Thirty feet from landing, the tail rotor on the helicopter just stopped dead. The body of the helicopter started to spin in all directions and we quickly thudded down. Hard. It wasn't a crash landing, but it was a heavy landing. That was my introduction to Woodstock."

Joe Cocker kicked off Sunday's music. The wonderfully spastic singer had his hands full with a distracted audience.

Joe Cocker: "I remember a guy shouting at me to 'look up there! Look at those clouds!' What a challenge! Y'know, it took us three quarters of a set to even get anybody's attention. I was looking at half a million people eating food, talking to one another, sunbathing and just enjoying themselves. And I'm trying to get them all to concentrate on the band. It took the entire set to get there. That's probably why I got so excited at the end. I think I was the only guy there that wasn't taking a bit of LSD that day."

So the sun is shining and Joe Cocker is rocking and there's these men sitting in a circle near me facing each other doing the hand jive. They all look alike, with big drooping mustaches, and I find it hysterically funny. Someone next to me offers up some hash in a handmade tin foil pipe and I breathe it in deeply, exhaling in a coughing spasm. The brown acid is starting to kick in. It seems that Joe won't stop singing "With A Little Help From My Friends" until all his friends in the audience rise as one and gives him the standing ovation, which he truly deserves.

I'm dancing and laughing and grooving hard, loving the brown acid. I thought I was hallucinating when overhead the sky got so damn dark in the middle of the day that I just kept looking upward, almost seeing a face in the clouds that looked like Elvis. That's when I noticed everyone else also looking up. It was a dramatic moment of a weekend that had—up to that point—been all fun and games. I was stoned to the bone, 18, wild and free. It felt great. I was with my people, they understood me, I understood them, they were feeding me, keeping me stoned, yet keeping me grounded. Foolhardy fans, in an effort to touch the sky, kept climbing up the light towers.

There was this couple ahead of me holding hands. They had divested themselves of all their clothing and stood there proudly naked. Then others started doing the same thing. I kept wishing Neil would come back already. I started thinking about all the sandwiches and, especially, the two filled canteens of what must have been hot water by now back in the car. Where was the car? Now I was getting paranoid. The announcement came that the music had to end. I equated it with life having to end. The music was all we had! Our situation had gone from bad to worse. Now there was no music and the heavens opened up.

I was madly tripping. Doing a little rain dance. Laughing. But I noticed people weren't laughing with me anymore. They were looking at me funny.

Joe Cocker felt like the only one at Woodstock not tripping on LSD.

And why were so many people naked? And where was Neil? Things were getting weird. It was coming down in buckets. My sense of being alone was heightened by loud claps of thunder and jagged streaks of lightning that brought oohs and aahs as if people were watching fireworks. I started to panic. My heart was beating out of my chest. I was soaked. I was hungry. I was thirsty. I had to go to the bathroom. There was no music. I had no idea what happened to Neil. I had no idea where the car was. I was still in the same shorts and T-shirt from Thursday. It was raining even harder now and everything was gray. I stood stone still looking at the strangers around me, trying to figure out how I could leave but what about Neil? Hell, we had maintained the same spot for

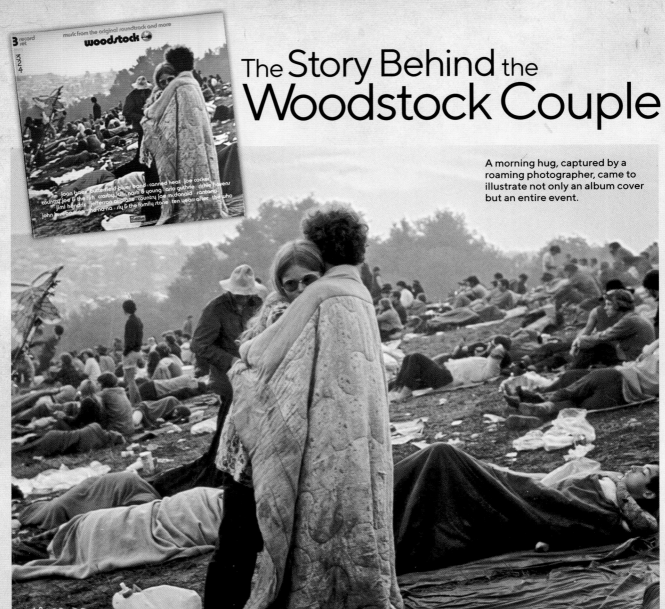

The Story Behind the
Woodstock Couple

A morning hug, captured by a roaming photographer, came to illustrate not only an album cover but an entire event.

music from the original soundtrack and more
woodstock
3 record set
324

joan baez · butterfield blues band · canned heat · joe cocker
country joe & the fish · crosby, stills, nash & young · arlo guthrie · richie havens
jimi hendrix · jefferson airplane · country joe mcdonald · santana
john sebastian · sha-na-na · sly & the family stone · ten years after · the who

WOO-33

"WOODSTOCK" A Film by MICHAEL WADLEIGH • Produced by BOB MAURICE • A WADLEIGH-MAURICE, Ltd. Production • TECHNICOLOR® From WARNER BROS.
COPYRIGHT © 1969 MAGNUM PHOTOS, INC. PHOTOGRAPHY BY CHARLES HARBUTT, BURK UZZLE AND ELLIOTT LANDY
COPYRIGHT © 1970 BY WARNER BROS. INC. ALL RIGHTS RESERVED. COPYRIGHT IS WAIVED TO MAGAZINES AND NEWSPAPERS. COUNTRY OF ORIGIN U.S.A. IMPRIME AUX ETATS-UNIS D'AMERIQUE.

Photo by Michael Ochs Archives/Getty Images

As Sunday morning broke, Nick and Bobbi Ercoline stood wrapped in a dirty quilt, embracing the new day at Max Yasgur's farm. Little did they realize theirs was an embrace that would last forever on the cover of the *Woodstock* album.

The couple had been dating for only a few months when they decided to ignore official warnings to stay away and to make the short drive over to Bethel. "When you're 20 years old and someone tells you not to do something, you're going to do it," Nick says today.

Photographer Burk Uzzle, strolling the festival grounds, came upon the snuggling pair, snapped a few pictures and moved on. After the festival, Bobbi and Nick returned to the routine of their world: he was a bartender/college student and she worked at a bank. "We didn't know the picture had been taken until the album came out," Bobbi says.

Uzzle's photo of the couple was used in a *New York* magazine pictorial and later selected for the cover of the *Woodstock: Music from the Original Soundtrack and More*, the best-selling, three-record album released May 1970. Quite by accident, the image of Nick and Bobbi came to define a quasi-mystical moment in time.

Of course, time keeps moving down the road, and so did the Pine Bush, New York, couple. Nick and Bobbi fell in love and married in August 1971. He became a union

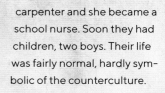

AP photo

carpenter and she became a school nurse. Soon they had children, two boys. Their life was fairly normal, hardly symbolic of the counterculture.

"It was exciting to see the album, but it wasn't a big deal – Woodstock was over," Bobbi said. "It wasn't until the 20th anniversary in 1989 that our story came out. *Life* magazine put an ad in our local paper looking for people who were there to come forward. I filled in the coupon and mailed it back, and a photographer arrived the following day."

The *Life* story went viral. Seemingly overnight, some twenty years later, The Woodstock Couple had names, faces and a wonderful story to share. And share they do. The couple has traveled overseas and been on Oprah; they Skype with schoolchildren from around the country and still receive items in the mail to be autographed several times a month. And of course, they return to where it all took root – Woodstock.

"This has given us so many wonderful memories and opportunities," Bobbi says. "The wonderfulness of it all is that we still love each other."

days. Right now, though, that spot was a lake. I was standing up; the mud was up past my ankles. No way could I sit back down. So I stood. And stared. It got real cold. I started shaking.

Someone hit me in the back and I went flying. When I got up to see who it was, I saw Neil's smiling face and he was holding bread! "Get up you idiot," he laughed, "you look like a mud pie."

"NEIL! WHERE WERE YOU?"

"I tried to find the car but gave up," he admitted. "Some nice people gave me this bread. Let's eat."

With Neil back, a full tummy and the music starting again, I forgot about my drenched clothing and tried to catch the rain in my mouth to drink. With the rain letting up a bit, the thought that we were all in this together made me happy. Things would be OK.

When the rain stopped and Country Joe & the Fish led the F-bomb cheer again, we relented and became one with the mud. There was nothing we could do about it anyway. So we sat in the wet brown ooze and reveled in it. Neil was a champ. Sober, wet, freezing, hungry and thirsty again, Neil suffered through the rest of the day because he knew I was caught up in the moment, and did not want to go. He was miserable and I knew it. And I finally figured out why people got naked during the rain. They were putting their clothes under their tarps to have dry clothing once the storm passed.

Then the cold really set in. It was freezing.

People started building fires. Guys who you'd be afraid to meet in a dark alley wound up taking charge and keep-

ing us all warm. I admit to being one of those who just stood around needing help. It got down to the point of basic prehistoric man essentials: fire, food, and water. And, of course, music. I remember feeling, as band after band took the stage, that the music was everything. As long as the music played, I was fine. Soon helicopters hovered. They were dropping something on us. Flowers. Millions of flowers.

As the sun set on the last day of the festival, Neil was dying to leave. "Oh no, another band," he'd snarl. I was still tripping. Heavily. That brown acid was a ballbuster. Still, I had to stay to see The Band and they didn't disappoint. And there was no way I was going to leave during Johnny Winter, who even got a rise out of Neil to rouse him out of his grumpiness. He was dying to leave. Finally, as Blood, Sweat & Tears took the stage, Neil said, "that's

Photo credit should read EMMANUEL DUNAND/AFP/Getty Images

Five hundred thousand people, 32 musical acts and three days filled with countless trials and triumphs. That's right, it leaves a mark.

Equal parts myth and controlled chaos, Woodstock was less about the music than it was the young people who clung to a moment that lasted a lifetime.

Photo by Ralph Ackerman/Getty Images

enough. Let's go. Now."

"But what about Jimi Hendrix," I meekly countered.

"Screw Jimi Hendrix," Neil yelled, and he was right.

As we walked and walked and walked, not knowing exactly where we were going but buoyed by an inner calm and plenty of food along the way from townspeople who were now out in force handing out all sorts of goodies, I'll never forget the feeling of total safety as we passed others along our way in the darkness of a magical forest festooned with Christmas lights. We flashed the peace sign to everyone we saw, saying hello, and getting directions back to the parking lot.

The finding of the car was like the finding of the Holy Grail and we tore into the food, the water, the dry clothes and although Neil wanted to leave immediately, he was nice enough to wait while I smoked one last joint.

Once we found the highway and were grooving to music on the radio, I told Neil that maybe we should pull over to the rest stop and get some sleep. The truth was that the radio music was sounding too good. I was too high to drive. Neil didn't have his license. He rolled his eyes but agreed. We fell asleep in the relative comfort of my car within minutes and awoke Monday late morning to a bright sunshine and clear sailing all the way home. I dropped Neil off at his house.

When I put my key in the lock of my front door, my mother pulled the door open from the inside, squished me to her bosom as she cried and cried and cried.

Wade Lawrence, museum director and senior curator at The Museum at Bethel Woods, Bethel, New York.

Emmanuel Dunand / AFP / Getty Images

AFTERWORD

WHEN THE MUSIC STOPPED

After the last note was played and the last piece of garbage was swept up, Woodstock expenses had climbed to around to $2.5 million, a hefty sum in 1969. After the concert, creditors descended on the business offices like buzzards on fresh road kill, scavenging for cash or certified checks among the bones. There was little to be found. Ironically, the biggest money-making venture connected to the event was the Academy Award-winning documentary directed by Michael Wadleigh, who was assisted by a team of editors that included Martin Scorsese and Thelma Schoonmaker. Released in 1970, *Woodstock*, the movie, provided a wonderfully kaleidoscopic concert experience without the rain, mud or acid of the real thing. Moviegoers had a better view of the goings-on than most of the actual concert attendees.

The film received widespread praise, including an Oscar for Best Documentary. With a production budget of just $600,000, the film grossed $50 million in the U.S., making it the sixth highest grossing film of 1970. Acclaimed film critic Roger Ebert included the documentary on his "Greatest Movies" list in 2005. What's more, the movie made stars out of the many of the concert performers. Country Joe McDonald says it enabled him to make a living for all the decades since as a solo artist.

Yet the peace and love continuum that permeated the proceedings at Woodstock did not translate into the post-event world of the original four—financiers John Roberts [1945-2001] and Joel Rosenman versus idea men Michael Lang and Artie Kornfeld. They grew to hate each other so much in the intervening years that lawsuits flew fast.

In fact, Roberts told Joel Makower in his 1989 *Woodstock: The Oral History*, "there were 10 or 12 years after the festival that I really despised him [Lang] and he didn't care for me, either. But I guess that comes with anything when you do something so tender and so touching and so raw emotionally. It's like a divorce. You come out with some bitter feelings."

The same can almost be said for Campground Coordinator Stanley Goldstein and Production Coordinator/Booker/Co-Host John Morris, two men who shared a common experience and who both proved essential to the festival's success. Goldstein accused Morris, in Makower's book, of staging an "attempt to cut everyone out but him as the promoter and producer of the event." Morris is incredulous to this accusation. "No, that's not true at all," he maintains. "It makes no sense. He was a good friend. That is not what I did. I think early on, we all started to have disagreements about

how things were being done. Michael [Lang] set up an office downtown which was counter to the one where John [Roberts] and Joel [Rosenman] were. He very much wanted to frame them out of the picture. I felt that since they were paying for it, they were the two who'd be responsible in the end for the financial aspects, therefore for the well being of everyone in those offices. We had things at that point that caused problems and disagreements. Michael and Artie [Kornfeld] had one attitude. Chris [Langhart], Josh [White] and I had another. It was to get it done, put on a good concert, and get it over with."

But Woodstock can never really be over with.

Wade Lawrence is a man who has dedicated his recent history to keeping the best of the Woodstock legend alive for generations to come. As museum director and senior curator at The Museum at Bethel Woods, Lawrence has come to realize that what went on right outside his office a half-century ago has greater implications than anyone could have originally envisioned.

Born in New Orleans and raised in Memphis, Lawrence studied architecture in Florida before earning a degree in art history from the University of Minnesota in 1984 and a degree in Early American Culture from the University of Delaware in 1987. Lawrence has been a student of American pop culture all his life. So maybe he can answer the question that still hovers over Woodstock like so much purple haze.

Why should anyone even care anymore about a concert so long ago and far away?

"If you talk to the people in the early to mid '70s the answer would be it isn't relevant or important," Lawrence says. "Within 10 years of the festival, it had become trivialized. A lot of people considered it quaint or passé because peace and love just doesn't exist in a gritty world. A cynicism had set in. There are those who point to Altamont [the violent Altamont Speedway Free Festival in December 1969] as proof. It was the age. Too much flower power became naïve and unworkable. Yet in talking to those who were there—I was in Memphis at the time—and those who participated in the counterculture, you hear that it was symbolic of the entire era. The 1960s was the decade with probably the most societal change ever in political views, fashion, music, where people lived, how people treated one another, the whole idea of equality expanding beyond just white men with property. It was a tumultuous exciting decade of change and Woodstock encapsulated it. It's the touchstone of that decade, a microcosm, if you will, of that decade."

The Museum at Bethel Woods serves to preserve, of course, but there's more. You see it as pilgrims of all ages trek through interactive exhibits and an era of change and promise, and even inspiration.

"If nothing else happens but inter-generational conversations, I'd be happy and would consider it a success," Lawrence says. "But it's even more than that. People get inspired to get involved in their own community by whatever means they find to be appropriate be it going out to vote, running for office, volunteering at school, cleaning up a park, protesting a nuclear plant, whatever. We don't try and tell people what to think but we do want people to think and express themselves. We try not to be political but we want to motivate people to be political on their own terms.

Image courtesy Heritage Auctions

Woodstock (Warner Brothers, 1970), movie poster.

yeah, it seemed to split on generational lines, and we touch on that. It has to be part of the story.

"But there's so much more. The idea that in the early '60s, you got your music from AM radio that had a set playlist derived from hit singles, thus we heard the same songs over and over. Songs about puppy love and surfing. Then Dylan, The Beatles and Byrds started singing about themes that mattered. Questioning things. FM radio became popular. Whole albums. FM became part of our social fabric.

"Sure, there were drugs. Pot, hashish and LSD were prevalent. The people who look down on that look at it from a moral standpoint and equate pot

"Vietnam divided families," Lawrence says. "Dinnertime was a battlefield in my house. My dad was very much 'America: Love It Or Leave It.' He supported the President. I believed the government was corrupt and we shouldn't be empire building in Vietnam. The two of us really didn't see eye-to-eye on that and I think it was repeated over and over across the country. The generations disagreed across the board. And even within the generation. Not all young people were against the war and not all old people were for the war. But,

with heroin. The era was about experimentation and finding one's self. Drugs were part of the equation. Not everybody was stoned at Woodstock. It was a reflection of society at the time. People who were going to get stoned would get stoned whether or not they were at Woodstock."

INVITED
TO THE DANCE BUT...

IT IS FASCINATING TO THINK OF THE 25 ACTS THAT MICHAEL LANG WANTED BUT FOR WHATEVER REASON DECLINED TO PERFORM AT WOODSTOCK.

Pjhoto by GAB Archives/Redferns

Tommy James and The Shondells were not the only acts to turn down a Woodstock invite.

1 THE BEATLES. Lang's efforts to get the Beatles back together for one more gig proved fruitless in the face of John Lennon's visa problems. **2 BOB DYLAN** opted to perform at The Isle Of Wight Festival off the coast of England just weeks later. **3 THE BYRDS. 4 CHICAGO. 5 THE DOORS.** Singer Jim Morrison was still facing legal problems for allegedly exposing himself onstage. Plus, he was a hopeless, helpless paranoid alcoholic by that time, prone to not even showing up. Lang knew this and still wanted them. When contacted by Lang's staff, he reportedly told his booking agent that he was afraid of being assassinated onstage. **6 DONOVAN. 7 FREE. 8 IRON BUTTERFLY.** Delayed at the airport on the way to the festival, their excessive rock star demands were then so out-of-line–despite being offered ten grand–that the offer was withdrawn. **9 JEFF BECK GROUP.** Rod Stewart was hellbent to go solo, thus breaking up the band, so they simply never showed up. Keyboardist Nicky Hopkins was so upset he went anyway and wound up playing with Jefferson Airplane. **10 JETHRO TULL.** According to leader Ian Anderson, "we were told that Woodstock was available for us to play shortly before the event. I asked a few questions about the nature of the festival and was told that there would be lots of drugs and naked hippies, neither of which held much appeal for me. And, it was too big an event-type show for Tull in our early days and we would have been forever branded with the 'Woodstock Band' tag." **11 JOHNNY CASH. 12 JONI MITCHELL.** Fearing she would miss a scheduled appearance on "The Dick Cavett Show," she declined. She wrote the song "Woodstock" instead. **13 LAURA NYRO.** Excessive stage fright prevented her from accepting. **14 LED ZEPPELIN** was already contracted for different shows. **15 LIGHTHOUSE. 16 LOVE.** Arthur Lee was feuding with his own band at the time. **17 MIND GARAGE. 18 MOODY BLUES.** Their '69 tour was completed and it would have cost the band more to travel to New York than what they were offered to play so they politely declined. **19 MOTHERS OF INVENTION.** Frank Zappa once famously said "too much mud" as the reason his band turned down the invite. **20 PROCOL HARUM.** Robin Trower's wife was pregnant. **21 RAVEN. 22 ROY ROGERS** was Michael Lang's first choice to close the festival by singing "Happy Trails To You." The cowboy refused. **23 SIMON & GARFUNKEL** simply hated each other too much to continue their '69 tour. **24 SPIRIT. 25 TOMMY JAMES & THE SHONDELLS.** "Yeah yeah I turned it down," says Tommy James today. "Sure, I regret it but can you blame me? We were playing Hawaii. We started out in Hilo, then had two weeks off before playing Honolulu. They put us up at this gorgeous Spanish villa mansion at the foot of Diamondhead, probably the most expensive piece of property in the United States. We were just hanging out. My secretary Joanne called me from my New York City office at Roulette Records. It was Tuesday of Woodstock week. 'Listen,' she says. 'Artie Kornfeld is here. He wants you to play this pig farm in Upstate New York.' Travel 6,000 miles from paradise to a farm in Upstate New York and then back again to make the next gig in Honolulu? I laughed in her face."

ABOUT
THE AUTHOR

All Mike Greenblatt has ever done in his entire life is listen to music and tell people about it, be it as a New York City publicist, editor or freelance journalist. It's been five decades of journalistically chronicling rock 'n' roll in all of its many permutations. Whether flying with Hank Williams, Jr. in his private jet, driving around the Jersey Shore with Bruce Springsteen, getting angrily thrown against a backstage wall by Meat Loaf, or being locked in a dressing room with Jerry Lee Lewis threatening to kill him, Greenblatt's voice—influenced by Nick Tosches, Henry Miller and James Ellroy—has yelled loud and long.

Greenblatt has interviewed Elton John, the Eagles (where he extemporaneously interviewed Joe Walsh at side-by-side urinals deep within the bowels of Giants Stadium), Paul McCartney, Blondie, The Allman Brothers, Waylon Jennings and hundreds of others. The author maintains his political demeanor and the state of musical Zen at concerts, is a direct result of his Woodstock experience.

Greenblatt lives in Easton, Pennsylvania with his music-teacher wife and their two rescue beagles. He is the proud parent of two and grandfather of two, yet still finds time to watch as much baseball as humanly possible.

ACKNOWLEDGEMENTS

Thanks to the following members of Woodstock Nation for adding their memories and insights: Jack Casady, Jefferson Airplane; John Chester, Fillmore East sound man; Doug Clifford, Creedence Clearwater Revival; Joe Cocker, 1982; Jacob Cohen, fan; Stu Cook, Creedence Clearwater Revival; Jerry Cordasco, fan; Rob Freeman, fan; Bob Goddard, Fillmore East crew; Larry Graham, Sly & The Family Stone, 1977; Henry Gross, Sha Na Na; Bill Hanley, ("The Father of Festival Sound"); Barry Hauser, fan; Richie Havens, 1984; Tommy James; Professor Chris Langhart; Wade Lawrence, curator, The Museum of Bethel Woods; Country Joe McDonald; Chip Monck, Lighting/Co-Host; John Morris, Production Coordinator/Booker/Co-Host; Graham Nash; Paul Nelson, Johnny Winter's manager; Willie Nile, fan; Fito De La Parra, Canned Heat; Amalie Rothschild, photographer; Carlos Santana; Michael Shrieve, Santana; Barry Schneier, fan; Scott Stoner, fan; Skip Taylor, Canned Heat manager; Edgar Winter; and Dr. Neil Yeager, fan.

Additional thanks to: Louise Barile Casapulla, Diane Casazza, Ellen Cooper, Dee Feldman, Gregg Geller, Andrew Greenblatt, Janet Kirk-Greenblatt, Elliot Horne (deceased), Michael Jensen, Gene Kalbacher (deceased), Carol Kaye, Paul Kennedy, Marla Kleman, Mike Palermo, Pat Prince, Jim Rensenbrink (deceased), Carol Ross, Bob Santelli, Bob Schartoff, Jessica Seeley, Kim Seeley, Susan Shapiro, Cary Silkin, Susan Sliwicki, Lari Thaw, Dawn Williams and Renee Young.

BIBLIOGRAPHY

Aquarius Rising: The Rock Festival Years, Robert Santelli, 1980, Delacorte Press

Back To The Garden: The Story of Woodstock and How It Changed A Generation, Pete Fornatale, 2009, Simon and Schuster

Barefoot in Babylon: The Creation of the Woodstock Music Festival 1969, Bob Spitz, 1979, Penguin Publishing Group

Bill Graham Presents: My Life Inside Rock and Out, Bill Graham and Robert Greenfield, 1992, Doubleday

Bruce, Peter Ames Carlin, 2012, Touchstone

Fortunate Son: My Life My Music, John Fogerty, 2015, Back Bay Books/Little, Brown and Co.

Long Time Gone: The Autobiography of David Crosby, David Crosby/Carl Gottlieb, 1988, Doubleday

The Road To Woodstock, Michael Lang with Holly George-Warren, 2009 Ecco/Harper-Collins Publishers

The Soundtrack Of My Life, Clive Davis, 2013, Simon & Schuster

Woodstock: Peace, Music & Memories, Brad Littleproud and Joanne Hague, 2009, Krause Publications/F+W Media

Woodstock: The Oral History, Joel Makower, 1989, Excelsior Editions/State University of New York Press, Albany

WELL, I CAME UPON A CHILD OF GOD
HE WAS WALKING ALONG THE ROAD
AND I ASKED HIM, TELL ME, WHERE ARE YOU GOING
THIS HE TOLD ME
SAID, I'M GOING DOWN TO YASGUR'S FARM
GONNA JOIN IN A ROCK 'N' ROLL BAND
GOT TO GET BACK TO THE LAND
AND SET MY SOUL FREE

"WOODSTOCK"
WRITTEN BY JONI MITCHELL
© SONY/ATV MUSIC PUBLISHING LLC

Stephen Stills and David Crosby,
of CSN&Y, onstage at Woodstock.

Photo by Fotos International/Getty Images